For Karen
See the pages about
~~Baptism~~ & Confirmation
(P. 127 & 136)

POCKET
CATHOLIC
CATECHISM

Feel free to
share this book
with family & friends
if you want!
you may find some
answers & insight
to Catholic
but may
even

Love, Kathryn
your Sponsor
& friend

D0951746

POCKET CATHOLIC CATECHISM

JOHN A. HARDON, S.J.

IMAGE BOOKS

Doubleday

New York London Toronto Sydney Auckland

AN IMAGE BOOK

PUBLISHED BY DOUBLEDAY

a division of Bantam Doubleday Dell Publishing Group, Inc.
1540 Broadway, New York, New York 10036

IMAGE, DOUBLEDAY, and the portrayal of a deer drinking
from a stream are trademarks of Doubleday, a division of
Bantam Doubleday Dell Publishing Group, Inc.

Imprimi Potest: Very Rev. Howard J. Gray, S.J.
Provincial
Detroit Province
December 1988

Nihil Obstat: Francis J. McAree, S.T.D.
Censor Librorum

Imprimatur: ✠ Rev. Msgr. Patrick J. Sheridan
Vicar General
Archdiocese of New York
December 6, 1988

The nihil obstat and imprimatur are official declarations
that a book or pamphlet is free of doctrinal error. No implication is contained therein that those who have granted the nihil
obstat and imprimatur agree with the contents, opinions, or
statements expressed.

Library of Congress Cataloging-in-Publication Data

Hardon, John A.
    Pocket Catholic catechism / by John A. Hardon.
—1st ed.
        p.   cm.
    "Image books."
    Includes index.
    ISBN 0-385-24293-X
    1. Catholic Church—Catechisms—English.   2. Apostles'
Creed.   3. Sacraments—Catholic Church.   4. Ten
commandments.   5. Lord's prayer.   I. Title.
BX1961.H367   1989
238'.2—dc19   88-25604
                                                          CIP

Copyright © 1989 by John A. Hardon

All Rights Reserved
Printed in the United States of America
April 1989
5   7   9   10   8   6   4

ACKNOWLEDGMENTS

My prayerful gratitude to Patricia Kossmann, editor of Image Books, for first suggesting the *Pocket Catholic Catechism* and for her generous cooperation in seeing the book through months of publication. Also to her collaborators and in a special way to the publishers of Doubleday.

To Carol Egan, Robert More, Gary Maloney, and Martha Prokop for their indispensable help in typing the manuscript.

To Geraldine Donovan for her expert work in proofreading the manuscript and the printed text.

To Dr. George Sharp and John Gonoud for their editing assistance.

To my Jesuit brethren for reading the manuscript and providing welcome observations on improving its contents.

I promise to remember at the altar these and the many others who have made the *Pocket Catholic Catechism* possible.

Contents

Contents

Contents

INTRODUCTION

As we begin our inquiry into the Catholic religion, it is important to explain briefly what we are about. Our purpose is very simple. We want to learn what the Catholic Church teaches her members should believe, where to obtain the help they need from God to live as faithful Christians, how He wants them to serve Him, and how they are to pray.

These four dimensions of the Catholic religion are as old as Christianity. They may be expressed in four words: faith, sacraments, commandments, and prayer. They are, in fact, the four pillars on which Jesus Christ built His Church and on which she has stood firm for two thousand years.

A word of explanation will be useful about each of these four pillars before we examine them in more detail.

The Catholic faith is what those who profess to belong to the Church are to believe: There are certain truths that the mind is to accept on the word of God. These truths are contained in concentrated form in the Apostles' Creed.

11

Introduction

The Catholic sacraments are the means that Christ provided for His followers in order to share in His own divine life, to grow in His life during their stay in this world, and, if necessary, to regain the divine life if it has been lost through sin.

The Ten Commandments are the main demands that God makes on our obedience to His will. They were first given to Moses on Mount Sinai, then confirmed and completed by Jesus Christ in His Sermon on the Mount. They are the conditions that God sets down for our sometimes painful submission to Him as our Creator, so we might return to Him as the eternal Destiny who will satisfy all our desires.

The Lord's Prayer is at once a summary and a guide. It summarizes all the ways we are to approach God as our loving Father in prayer. It also guides us in our conversation with Him, here on earth, as a preparation for our eternal communication with Him in heaven.

Scriptural references are from the *Latin Vulgate* and *The Jerusalem Bible*.

PART ONE

THE APOSTLES' CREED

THE BASIC PROFESSION OF FAITH

The Apostles' Creed was originally a profession of faith required of converts to Christianity before they were baptized. As a formula of belief, it goes back in substance, if not in words, to the twelve apostles.

Following Christ's declaration that "He who believes and is baptized will be saved" (Mark 16:16), the Apostles' Creed was the precondition for baptism. Only believers could be baptized. Even when children were baptized in the early Church, someone had to profess the faith for them.

Since the Apostles' Creed was first formulated, there have been many other creeds approved and used by the Church. But this creed still remains the most common profession of the Christian faith in the world.

There is no other place to start talking about Christianity than with the Christian faith. "Our faith," we are told, "can guarantee the blessings that we hope for and prove the existence of the realities that at present remain unseen" (Hebrews 11:1).

What the Apostles' Creed tells us is what everyone who calls himself a Christian must accept on the word of God, that is, on faith.

We accept three fundamental truths in the Apostles' Creed.

- We believe that the world did not always exist, but was created by God who existed from all eternity.

- We believe that God became man in the person of Jesus Christ, that He was born of the Virgin Mary, died on the cross and rose from the dead, and that He will return on the last day to judge the living and the dead.

- We believe that Christ sent His Holy Spirit, who is the soul of the Church which Christ founded, and that through the Church we receive all the graces we need to reach the eternal life for which we were made.

What needs to be emphasized is that belief in these revealed truths is the foundation of Christianity. We can hope only in what we know to be true; faith provides us with the guarantee that our hope is not in vain. We can love only what we know to be good; faith provides us with the vision that God is so good we should love Him with our whole heart and soul.

I.

"I Believe in God, the Father Almighty, Creator of Heaven and Earth"

The opening article of the Apostles' Creed is also the most fundamental: It lays the foundation for everything else we believe as Christians.

It is remarkable how many truths of faith are implied in the simple sentence, "I believe in God, the Father Almighty, Creator of heaven and earth." Each of these truths has been questioned in the course of the Church's history, and each is being challenged today. That is why as Catholics we have no choice in the modern world: We must know exactly what we profess in the first article of our Creed.

The method we plan to follow will be carried through the *Pocket Catholic Catechism*. After a short introduction, like the present one, we will look at a series of truths that underlie each principal area of our reflections, always attempting both to understand what we mean by what we believe, and how this faith should be lived out in actual practice.

Faith

To believe means to accept with our minds what someone tells us is true. We believe because we trust a person's knowledge, that he knows what he is saying, and his honesty in telling us what he knows. When the person we believe in is a human being, we call it human faith. When the one we believe in is God, we call it divine faith.

The expression, "I believe in God," therefore, has two meanings. We first of all *believe God* because we know from reason that God exists and that He, more than anyone else, should be believed. He can neither deceive, because He is all-good, nor be deceived, because He is all-knowing. But we also *believe in God* because we accept on His word all that He has revealed to us about Himself and about His will for the human race.

It is important to emphasize that our knowledge about God comes not only from faith in His own self-revelation. We can also know God from reason, by reflecting on the wonders of His creation. St. Paul could not have been clearer about the duty everyone has to know God from observing the world that He has made. Speaking of the pagans of his day, Paul insists that "what can be known about God is perfectly plain to them, since God Himself has made it plain. Ever since God has created the world, His everlasting power and deity—however invisible—have been there for the mind to see in the things that He has made. That is why such people are without excuse" (Romans 1:19–21).

Faith is, indeed, a form of knowledge. It is reasonable knowledge because we know from reason that God exists. We can also prove by reason that He has revealed Himself to us because of the miracles He performed to make His revelations credible to our minds. But faith provides us with superior knowledge, far above what we could ever know by our naked reason alone.

That is why a believing child of six is wiser than an unbelieving genius of sixty. Or, as St. Paul described the unbelievers of every generation, "the more they called themselves philosophers, the more stupid they grew" (Romans 1:22). Certainly it takes humility of mind to accept divine revelation, but the reward of faith is lucidity of mind for which there is no counterpart in human erudition.

Attributes of God

When we speak of God's perfections, we call them "attributes" because we attribute to Him such qualities as belong to the divine nature. Yet all the while we realize that these perfections in God only dimly correspond, in human language, to various properties in creatures.

In reality, the divine attributes are identical among themselves and with the divine nature. But in our human way of thinking there are different attributes because they are like the differences we see in creation, which itself is a manifestation of the indescribable greatness of God.

The Apostles' Creed gives only one attribute of God: that He is almighty. Since apostolic times, however, the Church has identified no less than fifteen divine attributes and, by now, a library of literature has been written to explain what they mean.

God is absolutely *one* because He is the only Being who must exist, and because there are not many gods (polytheism). He is not just one chief god (henotheism), nor merely the good god along with an evil god (Manichaeism).

He is the *true* God because He really exists and is not a figment of the imagination projecting our own fears or desires.

He is the *living* God whose life is His very essence. He is the being whose inward activity is identical with His nature.

He is *eternal* because in God there is nothing past, as if it were no longer; nothing future, as if it were not yet. In Him there is only "is," namely, the present. That is why when Yahweh first appeared to Moses in the burning bush and Moses asked Him for His name, God told him, "I Am Who Am" (Exodus 3:14).

God is *immense* because He is beyond all measurement. He encompasses everything, while He alone cannot be encompassed by anything.

He is *incomprehensible* because He is not limited in any way. God is not confined either in the manner of a body or of a created spirit.

God is *infinite* not only because He has no limitations, but because He has within Himself the plenitude of all perfection. He is all-knowing, all-powerful, and has absolute fullness of being.

God is *unique* because there neither is nor can there be another God. He must have no equal.

God is pure *spirit*. He has no body or spatial dimension. In our own language, He is a spiritual being who thinks and who wills. He knows and He loves. He is in the deepest sense a personal God, and not some impersonal force or cosmic energy.

God is totally *simple* because there are no components or parts in Him, like body and soul or substance and accidental properties. Thus Christ said of Himself, "I *am* the way, the truth and the life" (John 14:6).

God is *unchangeable* because He eternally possesses the fullness of being. There is nothing He can acquire that He does not already have, nor lose what He already has.

God is *transcendent* not only because He surpasses all other beings, but because He is completely distinct from the world. He is the Totally Other.

He is *perfectly happy* in and of Himself, without dependence on any other being for beatitude.

God is finally the most *sublime* because He is beautiful in the highest degree. Beauty is that which pleases when seen. That is why the Scriptures condemn those who are seduced by creatures: "They have taken things for gods. Let them know how much the Lord of these excels them, since the Author of beauty has created them" (Wisdom 13:3).

The Catholic Church speaks of the foregoing

attributes of God as internal, because they pertain to God as He is in Himself. In today's world, in which atheism is so prevalent, we must be clear in our understanding of who the one true God is.

However, we must also recognize what are called the relative attributes of God. These are the divine perfections in relation to the world He has made. Among these, the Apostles' Creed mentions only His omnipotence or almightiness. By this, we mean that He cannot do anything that would deny His nature, like tell a lie; nor can He act in a contradictory manner, like changing His mind.

We know, of course, that God is also omniscient because He knows all things past, present, and future. He is all-good because He wants only to benefit the creatures that He makes. And He is even all-merciful in forgiving human beings, provided they repent for the offenses they have committed against their loving Lord.

The Holy Trinity

Our Christian faith tells us that God is not a solitary being. He is the eternal community of three Divine Persons: Father, Son, and Holy Spirit. Every society outside of God, whether among the angelic hierarchy or among human beings, exists only because of the Holy Trinity.

Revelation tells us that there is in God a true fatherhood that belongs to the First Person alone. From all eternity, the First Person has been generating the Son, who is not a mere attribute of God, but a distinct Person. This is clear from the opening words of the Fourth Gospel: "In the beginning was *the* Word, and the Word was with God, and the Word was God" (John 1:1). Proceeding from the Father and the Son is the Holy Spirit.

In the language of the *Credo of the People of God,* "The natural bonds which eternally constitute the Three Persons, who are each one and the same Divine Being, are the blessed inmost life of God, thrice holy, infinitely beyond all that we can conceive in human measure. We give thanks, however, to the Divine Goodness that very many believers can testify with us before men to the unity of God, even though they know not the mystery of the Most Holy Trinity."

We Christians are specially blessed in believing that there is only one God, but also that He is a triune plurality. Our destiny is to share in the happiness of this heavenly society.

At this critical period of humanity, the world is more socially conscious than ever before in history. Christianity offers today's believers both a timeless and timely understanding of the Trinity as the perfect model for living in a loving community.

Creation and Providence

In the Apostles' Creed we affirm that God is the Creator of heaven and earth. Saying this, we profess that He made the world out of nothing. He started with nothing, out of which He created the world, and He parted with nothing of Himself to bring the world into actual being.

Consequently, the world had a beginning. This is repeatedly stated in the Old Testament. "Aeons ago," the Psalmist tells the Lord, "you laid the earth's foundations, the heavens are the work of your hands" (Psalm 102:25). And St. Paul praises God the Father because "Before the world was made, He chose us, chose us in Christ" (Ephesians 1:4).

God did not have to create the world. The cause of all that He created is His divine and loving will. No necessity to create arises from God's goodness. It is true that the desire for self-communication belongs to the nature of goodness, but this is perfectly fulfilled within the Trinity by the mutual self-giving by each of the Three Divine Persons. God's goodness is, of course, the reason why He communicates of His being to creatures. But He does this of His own free will and without compulsion even by His own great love.

All Three Persons are equally and uniquely the Creator of the universe. As the work of creation, however, shows a similarity with the properties of the First Person it is usually referred to the Father by "appropriation." Thus in the Apostles' Creed.

Yet in referring creation to God the Father, we are also professing belief in the fatherly providence of the Holy Trinity. Providence is the all-wise plan of God for the universe, and the carrying out of this plan by His loving rule or governance.

Our response to divine Providence is to see in

every person, place, and event in our lives the providential hand of God. Everyone and everything in every moment is a manifestation of His providential care. He wants us to enjoy or endure, to remove or sacrifice some creature by which He intends to lead us to our eternal destiny.

Angels and Human Beings

It is the common teaching of the Church that God created angels and human beings. In the early thirteenth century, the Church had to formulate the Lateran Creed (1215) to defend the faith against the Albigenses, who claimed there were two gods. The good god created spiritual beings, while the evil god created the material world. The Lateran Creed declares:

> We firmly believe and profess without qualification that there is only one true God . . . the Father, the Son, and the Holy Spirit . . . They are the one and only principle of all things—Creator of all things visible and invisible, spiritual and corporeal. By His almighty power from the very beginning of time, He has created both orders of creatures in the same way out of nothing, the spiritual or angelic world and the corporeal or visible universe. And afterwards He formed the creature man, who in a way belongs to both orders, as he is composed of spirit and body. For the devil and other demons were created by God

25

good according to their nature, but they made themselves evil by their own doing. As for man, his sin was at the prompting of the devil (Fourth Lateran Council, 1215).

It will be useful to number the statements of faith professed in this important creed:

1. Only one God created the entire universe, spiritual and material, angelic and human.

2. This one God the Creator is the Holy Trinity, by whose almighty power all things came into existence.

3. Time began with the creation of the world. Why? Because time is the measure of change, and only with the origin of creatures did change come into being.

4. First God created the spiritual world of angels, who are persons with an intellect and will; then the material world, which is perceptible only to the senses.

5. Afterwards, God created man, who is like the angels in being able to think and to love, and like the tangible world of matter on which he walks and which he breathes. Man's soul is spiritual and naturally immortal; his body is material and naturally mortal.

6. The devil (Greek = *diabolos*, slanderer) and demons (Greek = *daimon*, evil god) were originally good angels. Proudly refusing to obey God,

they were cast into hell. They became evil by the misuse of their free wills.

Seven centuries after the Lateran Creed, Pope Pius XII returned to the subject of man's origin. In the meantime, various theories of evolution posed the question of how the human race began. According to the pope (*Humani generis*, August 12, 1950), "The teaching of the Church leaves the teaching of evolution an open question, as long as it confines its speculations to the development, from living matter already in existence, of the human body. The Catholic faith obliges us to hold that souls are immediately created by God."

In the same document, Pius XII took issue with those who espouse the theory of polygenism. Proponents of this theory claim that since evolution is an established fact, all human beings now on earth do not descend from one human pair, but from different human ancestors. These "conjectures about polygenism . . . leave the faithful no such freedom of choice. Christians cannot lend their support to a theory which involves the existence, after Adam's time, of some earthly race of men, truly so-called, who were not descended ultimately from him, or else supposes that Adam was the name given to some group of primordial ancestors."

In technical language, only monogenism (*mono* = one) and not polygenism (*poly* = many + *genus* = race) is compatible with the Catholic faith.

Original Sin

There was no major dissent from the biblical teaching about the fall of Adam until the rise of Pelagianism in the last part of the fourth century. Pelagius denied that Adam was endowed with the supernatural life of grace, which he lost for himself and his descendants by his sin of disobedience. To counteract this error, a series of Church councils were held. Not only was Pelagius condemned, but several popes confirmed the Catholic doctrine on original sin, stating:

1. Adam was the first man. He was created immortal. His bodily death was a punishment for sin (Pope Zozimus I, 418).

2. Adam's sin was injurious not only to Adam, but also to his descendants. Moreover, it was not only the death of the body, which is punishment for sin, but sin, the death of the soul, that passed from one man to all the human race (Pope Boniface II, 531).

A thousand years later, the Protestant reformers brought back Pelagius's ideas. As a result, the Council of Trent issued its famous *Decree on Original Sin.* Published in the same year (1546) that Martin Luther died, the conciliar definitions spell out in the plainest language what the Catholic Church teaches on this fundamental mystery of our faith:

Loss of Original Justice. "The first man Adam immediately lost the justice and holiness in which he was constituted when he disobeyed the command of God in the Garden of Paradise."

Death and Subjection to the Devil. "Through the offense of this sin he incurred . . . the death with which God had previously threatened him and, together with death, bondage in the power . . . of the devil" (Canon 1).

Communication and Remission of Original Sin. "This sin of Adam, which is one by origin, and which is communicated to all men by propagation . . . is taken away through [no other remedy] than the merit of the one mediator, our Lord Jesus Christ, who reconciled us to God in His blood" (Canon 3).

Baptism Confers Merits of Christ. "Through the sacrament of baptism rightly conferred in the form of the Church, this merit of Christ is . . . applied to adults and infants alike" (Canon 3).

Concupiscence Remains After Baptism. "Concupiscence or the tendency to sin remains in the baptized; but since it is left to provide a trial, it has no power to injure those who do not consent and who, by the grace of Christ Jesus, manfully resist" (Canon 5).

In the light of the foregoing, we see that our first parents were originally gifted three times over:

- They had the natural gifts of human beings, especially the power to think and to choose freely.

- They had the preternatural gifts of bodily immortality and of integrity, or the internal power to control their desires.

- They had the supernatural gifts of sanctifying grace, the virtues of faith, hope, and charity, and the corresponding title to enter heaven.

By their willful disobedience, they lost the supernatural and preternatural gifts entirely, and were weakened (without losing) their natural capacity to reason and to choose freely.

As we shall see at greater length later on, baptism restores the supernatural life lost by Adam's sin. It does not restore the preternatural gifts but gives us a title to a glorified restoration of our bodies on the last day, and a corresponding title to the graces we need to cope with our disorderly desires. Our natural powers of reason and free will remain weakened. But with God's grace, they are strengthened to enable us actually to become more holy through our struggle with concupiscence.

II.

"AND IN JESUS CHRIST, HIS ONLY SON, OUR LORD"

The second article of the Apostles' Creed follows logically on the first. Once we realize that mankind lost God's friendship at the dawn of human history, the coming of Christ takes on a profound meaning.

We believe that God became man in the person of Jesus Christ. We do not know whether the Incarnation would have taken place if man had not sinned. But we are sure that the Incarnation did take place because sin entered the world through Adam. In other words, the basic reason for the Incarnation is the need for man's redemption.

Our focus in looking at the second article of the Creed will be very exact. We will consider, in sequence, each of four terms, namely, Jesus, Christ, Son of God, and our Lord.

Jesus

The New Testament origins for the name *Jesus* are associated with two events in the gospels, the Annunciation of Mary and the revelation to St. Joseph.

At the Annunciation, the Angel Gabriel appeared to our Lady and addressed her as "full of grace." She was disturbed by these words. So the angel reassured her. "Mary, do not be afraid," he said. "You have won God's favor. Listen! You are to conceive and bear a son, and you must name him Jesus" (Luke 1:30–31).

Some time later, Gabriel again appeared, but this time to St. Joseph, who was understandably worried because Mary, his betrothed, had mysteriously conceived. Jewish law required that he put her away, yet he decided to do so quietly in order to spare her publicity. The angel told him: "Joseph, son of David, do not be afraid to take Mary home as your wife, because she has conceived what is in her by the Holy Spirit. She will give birth to a son and you must name Him Jesus, because he is the one who is to save his people from their sins" (Matthew 1:20–21).

The name "Jesus" is the Latin form of the Greek *Iesous*, whose Hebrew is *Yeshua*, which means "Yahweh is salvation." Already in the Book of Genesis, after our first parents had sinned, God promised to send a Redeemer. Addressing the devil, He said: "I will put enmity between you and the woman, between your seed and her seed; she shall crush your head and you shall lie in wait for her heel" (Genesis 3:15).

The seed of the woman, whom we identify with Mary, was to be descended from Adam. This same promise of a Redeemer was to be repeated many times in the Old Testament. And always the stress was on Yahweh as the one who saves. When it appears that He will not save, there is no one else who can save (Psalm 18:42). Yahweh alone saves (Hosea 13:4). The frequently occurring phrases "God of my (your, his) salvation" and "rock of my (your, his) salvation" are simply variants of the same basic theme. So often is Yahweh invoked or described by titles which use the words "save" and "salvation" that these can be called His most characteristic titles in the Old Testament.

This emphasis on Yahweh's saving power dramatically attests that the Incarnation was far more clearly predicted in the Jewish prophets than the rejection of Jesus by the Jewish leaders might seem to indicate. Time and again, without ceasing, the Old Testament insists that only God can save. Logically, then, God would become man to save His people from their sins.

Christ

The name "Christ" is taken from the Greek *Christos,* which means "Anointed." It corresponds exactly to the Hebrew *Mashiah* or Messiah.

Anointing was the normal way in which kings, priests, and sometimes prophets were invested with special powers by God for the exercise of their office among the people of Israel.

In what sense was Jesus anointed? He was not anointed by any mortal hand or with earthly ointment. He was anointed by the power of His heavenly

Father with such fullness of the Holy Spirit as no mere created being could receive. We may, therefore, say that the humanity of Jesus was anointed with the Divinity. As a result, the human nature of Jesus was hypostatically—that is, personally—united with the Divinity. Yet all the while, the human nature of Jesus remained truly human. It was and is human like ours, in everything but sin.

Even as prophets, priests, and kings were anointed with material oil, so Jesus was anointed with the spiritual oil which conferred on Him the fullness of prophetic, priestly, and royal power.

Jesus was and is the great Prophet (Greek *prophetes* = one who teaches or speaks for another). He is the Teacher, as He called Himself, whose human lips and actions reveal to us the mind and will of God.

Jesus was and is the great High Priest who sacrificed Himself on the Cross for our salvation. He continues to offer Himself in the Holy Sacrifice of the Mass.

Jesus was and is the King who has authority to govern and direct not only Christian believers, but the whole human race. When during his Passion Pilate asked Him, "So you are a King then," Jesus answered: "Yes, I am a King. I was born for this; I came into the world for this; to bear witness to the truth; and all who are on the side of truth listen to my voice" (John 18:37). Jesus was saying more than meets the eye. He is King, indeed, because He is the divine Ruler of the world in human form. But His rule is not coercive. We must voluntarily hear His commands, which means *listening* to His voice, if we are humbly to submit to His words.

Son of God

The Apostles' Creed wisely places the profession of faith in Jesus as the *Son of God* before going on to declare that He was born of the Virgin Mary. No single mystery of Christianity has been more widely and militantly opposed than the unqualified Divinity of Christ. We may say that everything else depends on this.

The key words are "His only Son," where each word has been chiseled out of the conflict between orthodox and heterodox Christian teaching. By the middle of the fifth century, the Church was ready to formulate her belief in the unique divine sonship of Jesus of Nazareth. Already at the Annunciation, the angel had told Mary that the child she was to conceive would be called "Son of the Most High."

From the Annunciation on, learned voices were raised to explain away the literal meaning of the angel's message to Mary. Strange names like Arius and Nestorius, Eutyches and Sabellius, Priscillian and Apollinaris are identified with heresies that in one way or another qualified Christ's true Divinity. By the middle of the fifth century our familiar Nicene Creed was formulated, which stated in clear language what this unique sonship of Jesus Christ really means.

The Nicene Creed declares: "We believe . . . in one Lord Jesus Christ, the only-begotten Son of God, born of the Father before all time; Light from Light, true God from true God; begotten, not created, consubstantial with the Father; through Him all things were made."

Because of the critical importance of this mystery of faith, it will be worth looking more closely at every term on the subject in the Nicene Creed.

The Only-Begotten Son of God. Jesus Christ had a natural human mother, Mary. But he had no natural human father. St. Joseph was not the natural father of Jesus. The natural father of Jesus is the First Person of the Holy Trinity, who is God the Father. Certainly we are all children of God, who is our Creator-Father. Certainly God is also the Father of our supernatural life, which we received at baptism. The essence of fatherhood is to share the same nature with its offspring. None of us is the natural son of God either by creation—when we were conceived in our mother's womb—or by baptism—when we were born into the life of grace. The best we can call ourselves is "adopted children of God."

Eternal Generation of the Son of God. The First Person of the Trinity never began to generate the Second Person. The Son has always proceeded from the Father, and will continue to do so for all eternity. This is *so* true, that all other generations of human offspring by their earthly fathers take place only because there is in God Himself the everlasting generation of the Son from the Father.

36

Light from Light. In the text of the Nicene Creed we profess at Mass are the expressions, "God from God, Light from Light, True God from True God." This is to declare how totally the nature of the Son is identical with the nature of the Father from whom He proceeds. The one proceeding is equally God, equally true God, equally one as light is identical with its originating light.

Begotten, Not Made. Our faith insists that the Second Person is not made by the Father because the Son is not created out of nothing. Rather, He is begotten of the Father. Why? Because He is "one in Being with the Father." At the Council of Nicea, the Greek word *homoousios* was coined to state in the clearest possible terms that the Son has the self-same (*homo*) Being (*ousia*) as the Father.

Through Him All Things Were Made. Since the Son is one in Being with the Father, He is equally Creator with the Father. This is stated in the opening words of St. John's Gospel. "Through Him," that is, through God "all things came to be, not one thing had its being but through Him" (John 1:2–3). Thus the whole created universe depends on the Son, who is the Wisdom of the Father, no less than it depends on the Father, who is Almighty Power.

Our Lord

In the light of what we have discussed, there can be no doubt why Jesus Christ is our Lord:

- He is our Lord because He is true God, the Creator of the universe.

- He is our Lord because, as God, He sustains us and the whole world by His loving omnipotence.

- He is our Lord because He continually provides for all our bodily and spiritual needs.

- He is our Lord because He governs the universe, including our own personal world, by His infinitely wise laws.

- He is our Lord because He is leading us every moment of our stay on earth to the eternal home which He has prepared for us in heaven.

III.

"Who Was Conceived by the Holy Spirit, Born of the Virgin Mary"

So far, the Apostles' Creed has identified Jesus Christ as the Second Person of the Trinity who became man. In this third article, we profess our belief in how Jesus became man. He was not conceived by a human father, but by the Holy Spirit; and He was born of the Virgin Mary.

Our concern here will be to see how the Church understands the humanity of Christ, and to identify the main privileges of His Mother, Mary. After all, it was from her that Jesus took His human nature, and she is still His Mother now with Him in heavenly glory.

Jesus Christ Is True Man

The oldest creeds of faith mention the most important facts of the earthly life of Jesus, namely, His conception and birth, His suffering and dying on the Cross, and His bodily resurrection from the dead. The language used is always about a Person who was one with the Father as God, but also one with us as man.

Already in apostolic times, the heresy of Docetism held that Christ only *seemed* to be a man, to be born, have lived, suffered, and risen from the dead. The Docetists were infected with the false philosophy which claimed that matter and spirit are totally opposed to each other. Consequently, it was said to be impossible that God, who is pure spirit, would become incarnate in a material body.

That is why St. John's Gospel is so clear in teaching that Jesus Christ is indeed one with the Father, who is God, and at the same time so insists on showing that Jesus Christ is true man.

Jesus became tired (John 4:6); He was in great distress (John 11:33); He wept at the tomb of Lazarus (John 11:35); He allowed His feet to be anointed (John 12:3); He washed the feet of His disciples (John 13:12); He was seized and bound in the Garden of Olives (John 18:12); He was slapped in the face by one of the guards during the Passion (John 18:22); He was scourged, crowned with thorns, and dressed in a purple robe (John 19:1–2); He carried His own Cross to Calvary (John 19:17); On the Cross, He said, "I am thirsty" and, after taking some vinegar from the soaked sponge held up to his mouth, He bowed His head and died (John 19:29–30); His side was pierced with a soldier's lance, and immediately there flowed out blood and water (John 19:34); After His resurrection, He invited the doubting Thomas to put his fingers into the holes made by the nails in His hands and to put his hand into His open side (John 20:27).

Human Body and Soul. There is more than passing value in knowing that Christ had a truly human body and soul.

- Because He had a human body and soul, they could be separated—as they were on the Cross—and thus cause His death.

- Because He had a human body and soul, He truly suffered in both, and thus redeemed us by enduring both bodily and spiritual pain.

- Because He had a human body and soul, when He rose from the dead He was reunited in body and soul.

- Because He had a human body and soul, He can be truly imitated by us in our striving after sanctity. The virtues He practiced as man were the attributes of God in human form. As we become more like Jesus in His life as man, the more we become like Jesus who is our God.

- Because He now has a glorified human body and soul, He is in the Holy Eucharist in the fullness of His human nature united with the Second Person of the Trinity in one Divine Person.

Human Free Will. The true humanity of Jesus implies that He had a free human will. It was because of this that He could merit our redemption. By the willing sacrifice of His life on the Cross, He won for us the graces we need for our salvation.

Sacrifice means the willing surrender to God of something precious. Jesus made this surrender by His own free human will, voluntarily offering Himself on Calvary to expiate our sins and save us for heaven and from hell.

While saying this, we dare not forget that, although He could really choose with a real human will, yet He could never sin. Not only did He not, but He could not sin because His human nature was united with His Divine nature in one Person who is God. And God cannot sin. The implications of this mystery are practical in the extreme. It does not belong to the essence of human freedom to be able to choose what is contrary to God's will. Jesus Christ could choose with His human will. In fact, He did so. But His choices were always what was most pleasing to His heavenly Father.

The struggle He experienced in His agony in the Garden was never a conflict of His free will with the will of the Father. It was the spontaneous dread a human being experiences when faced with the prospect of pain.

The Historical Jesus. A resurgent Docetism in modern times tries to reduce the historical facts about Jesus to mystical or even mythical ideas about Jesus. That is why we hear so much nowadays about the difference between the Jesus of history and the Christ of faith.

Early Christian believers, so the argument runs, were so hypnotized by the wonderful man Jesus that they made Him out to be more than He actually was. Their fervent imagination made Him into a Divine Person, and their pious fancy credited Him with all kinds of humanly impossible deeds. These ideas are at the root of what Pope St. Pius X condemned (*Lamentabili,* July 3, 1907) as Modernism. Some of the statements that the pope rejected are worth quoting in full:

1. "The divinity of Jesus Christ is not proved from the gospels. It is rather a dogma which the Christian conscience has deduced from the notion of a Messiah."

2. "It may legitimately be granted that the Christ whom history presents is far inferior to the Christ who is the object of faith."

3. "A critic cannot affirm that Christ's knowledge was unrestricted by any limit, except by making a supposition that is historically inconceivable and that contradicts moral sense."

4. "Christ did not always have the consciousness of His messianic dignity."

The Catholic Church has never allowed her followers to say that the creative imagination of the early believers adorned the original facts about Jesus. On the contrary, the Second Vatican Council (*Dei Verbum,* V, 19) issued an uncompromising statement about the historical validity of the gospels: "Holy

Mother the Church," the council declared, "has firmly and with absolute constancy held and continues to hold that the four gospels . . . whose historical character the Church unhesitatingly asserts, faithfully hand on what Jesus Christ, while living among men, really did and taught for their eternal salvation until the day He was taken up into heaven."

The key word in the Council's teaching is "really." This recalls what St. Peter wrote to the first-century Christians when he told them: "It was not any cleverly invented myths that we were repeating when we brought you the knowledge of the power and the coming of our Lord Jesus Christ." Why not? Because "we had seen His majesty for ourselves" (II Peter 1:16).

It also recalls what St. Ignatius wrote on his way to martyrdom in 107 A.D. "Jesus Christ," he said, "is *really* of the line of David according to the flesh . . . He was *really* nailed to the Cross in the flesh for our sake . . . He suffered *really*, and He also *really* raised Himself from the dead. It is not as some unbelievers say . . . In reality, it is they that are make-believers" (*Letter to the Smyrneans*, 1–2).

In today's skeptical age, when, for many, the historical foundations of Christianity are being reduced to myths, we must be able to see those who would demythologize the gospels for what they really are: They are make-believers.

The Blessed Virgin Mary

Our Lady is mentioned in the Apostles' Creed only in reference to her giving birth to Jesus Christ. This is consistent with the few passages in the New Testament that speak of the Blessed Virgin.

Yet Mary's place in Catholic faith and piety grew immensely through the centuries, and Marian piety has also been one of the principal areas of development of doctrine in the Catholic Church in modern times. Two solemn Marian definitions in less than a century. Two Marian years for the universal Church in one generation. Two major Marian shrines with millions of pilgrims annually from every part of the world—approved by the Church again in less than a century. Twelve papal encyclicals on the Rosary alone by four sovereign pontiffs. And a library of Marian literature that has no counterpart in all previous Catholic history. All these are some indication of what has been rightly called "The Age of Mary." In God's providence, Mary is meant to be venerated, we may safely say, as she has never been before.

All of this presumes that our Marian faith keeps pace with our devotion. In the words of the Second Vatican Council,

> Let the faithful remember that true devotion consists neither in sterile or transitory affection, nor in a certain vain credulity, but proceeds from true faith, by which we are led to recognize the

excellence of the Mother of God, and we are moved to a filial love toward our Mother and to the imitation of her virtues (*Constitution on the Church*, VIII, 67).

Mother of God.   Since apostolic times, it was assumed that since Jesus Christ is true God, Mary must be the Mother of God. But in the early fifth century, a heresy arose that claimed that Christ not only had two natures, but that He was two persons, one human and the other divine. Named after Nestorius, the patriarch of Constantinople, Nestorians were willing to call Mary the Mother of Christ (*Christotokos*) because she conceived and gave birth to the human person of Christ. But they refused to say she is the Mother of God (*Theotokos*). The Council of Ephesus (431) condemned Nestorianism, declaring unhesitatingly that we should call "the holy Virgin Mother of God."

Nestorian bishops, however, continued to propagate their views. The confusion this produced among the people contributed to the success of Islam among Christians in the seventh century. Islam, as we know, considers Jesus a great prophet, even the Messiah. He is called the "son of Mary" (*Ibn Maryam*), but according to Mohammed, Jesus may not be called "Son of God" (*Ibn Allah*). To this day, Moslems identify Christians as those who venerate Mary as the Mother of God.

Every aspect of Marian faith in Christianity rests on this premise: that Mary gave her Son all that any human mother gives the fruit of her womb. Since the

Child she conceived and gave birth to was a Divine Person, she must be honored as the Mother of God. History confirms this judgment. Where belief in Mary's divine maternity is professed, faith in her Son's Divinity remains intact.

Immaculate Conception. Mary's conception without original sin was a logical preparation for her divine maternity. Since the Child she was to bear would be the All-Holy God, it was unthinkable that His Mother would ever have been stained with sin.

From earliest times, the Fathers of the Church—like St. Irenaeus in the second century, St. Cyprian in the third century—wrote of Mary as not only immaculate but entirely immaculate, not only spotless but most spotless, that she alone was to be the dwelling place of all the graces of the Holy Spirit, because she was predestined to become the dwelling place of the Son of the Most High.

It was not surprising, then, that in 1854, Pope Pius IX proclaimed the following definition: "The most holy Virgin Mary was, in the first moment of her conception, by a unique gift of grace and privilege of Almighty God, in view of the merits of Jesus Christ the Redeemer of mankind, preserved from all stain of original sin."

This means that from the first moment of her existence, Mary was preserved from the common defect of lacking supernatural life. She possessed sanctifying grace from the moment she was conceived. She also possessed the virtues of faith, hope, and charity, and the gifts of the Holy Spirit.

Absolute Sinlessness. Consistent with the privilege of her Immaculate Conception, Mary was also preserved from all sin. This says more than at first may seem to be implied. Not only did she never actually offend God by even the slightest sin, but she was specially protected from committing sin.

Moreover, since our Lady was conceived without original sin, she was preserved from the one consequence of this sin that all of us so painfully experience. She did not have concupiscence or the unruly desires that are the heritage of all other descendants of man's original estrangement from God.

Perpetual Virginity. Mary's virginity is expressed in the Apostles' Creed. St. Luke states that "the angel Gabriel was sent from God . . . to a virgin . . . and the virgin's name was Mary" (Luke 1:26–27).

Mary's virginal conception of Jesus was already foretold in the Old Testament. Isaiah predicted the coming Messiah in a famous prophecy, declaring that "the Lord himself shall give a sign . . . Behold the virgin [Hebrew *alma,* Greek *parthenos*] shall conceive and bear a son and his name shall be called Emmanuel" (Isaiah 7:14).

From the early days of the Church, this prophecy was understood to refer to Mary's virginal conception of her Son, and St. Matthew's Gospel so interprets the words of Isaiah (Matthew 1:23). Nor was there any question among Christ's faithful believers but that Mary was a perpetual virgin.

Against those few individuals who denied Mary's

unimpaired virginity, St. Basil (329–379) wrote, "The friends of Christ do not tolerate hearing that the Mother of God ever ceased to be a virgin." Ambrose (339–397) wrote a whole treatise defending "the perpetual virginity of the Blessed Mary." And Pope St. Siricius in 392 simply declared that Mary was a "perpetual virgin."

Bodily Assumption into Heaven. Since our Lady was conceived without sin, she was not subject to the universal penalty of sin, which is bodily death.

The early tradition about Mary's departure from this world is especially strong in Eastern Christianity. We have records of the celebration of the Dormition (the Falling Asleep of Mary) from the end of the seventh century. The original title, Dormition, was changed into Assumption in the Gregorian Sacramentary, sent by Pope Hadrian I (790) to Emperor Charlemagne as the liturgical standard to be used in Charlemagne's empire. By the end of the eighth century, the Feast of the Assumption was celebrated universally in the West on August 15. And, in 847, Pope Leo IV ordered that an octave of the feast should also be observed.

The modern impetus for promoting the definition of Mary's bodily assumption into heaven belongs to St. Anthony Claret (1807–1870), founder of the Claretians and bishop of Santiago in Cuba. Thousands of petitions from all parts of the world were sent to Rome asking the pope to define Mary's assumption into heaven.

Finally, in 1946, Pope Pius XII addressed an official query to all the Catholic bishops in the Church. "Do you," he asked them, "in view of the wisdom and prudence that is yours, judge that the bodily assumption of the Blessed Virgin can be proposed and defined as a dogma of faith; and do you, along with your clergy and faithful, desire it?"

Within months, the pope received an almost unanimous reply in the affirmative. Consequently, on November 1, 1950, Pope Pius XII issued the solemn definition which stated:

> By the authority of our Lord Jesus Christ, of the Blessed Apostles Peter and Paul, and by Our Own authority, we pronounce, declare, and define as divinely revealed dogma: The Immaculate Mother of God, Mary ever Virgin, after her life on earth, was assumed body and soul to the glory of heaven.

The grounds for defining Mary's assumption as a dogma, or revealed doctrine, were Sacred Tradition as a co-equal source of divine revelation, along with Sacred Scripture. One reason for the definition was expressed by the pope when he spoke to the assembled four hundred bishops the day after the definition. He expressed the hope that this new honor to Mary would introduce "a spirit of penance to replace the prevalent love of pleasure, and a renewal of family life stabilized where divorce was common, and made fruitful where birth control was practiced."

Our Lady's bodily assumption should be a powerful motive for control of our bodily passions. Why?

Because after the last day, we are due to be rewarded with a glorified body for the merit we have gained during our life on earth in sacrificing sinful pleasures of the senses in obedience to the will of God.

Devotion to the Blessed Virgin.   As spelled out in the Second Vatican Council, devotion to the Mother of God is really a composite of three elements: veneration, invocation, and imitation. They belong together and may only be separated at the risk of detracting from the honors due to Mary, and depriving ourselves of the graces God wishes to confer on humanity through His beloved Mother.

Veneration of the Blessed Virgin includes all the honor and praise, recognition and love that she deserves as the Mother of the Redeemer and Mother of the human race. Veneration may be described as loving appreciation. The appreciation is based on the knowledge we have of Mary, based on the truths taught us by faith. The love is inspired by the depth of our appreciation, which depends on reading, study, and meditation about the Blessed Virgin Mary.

The first seven parts of the Hail Mary are all statements of veneration:

—Hail Mary

—Full of grace

—The Lord is with thee.

—Blessed art thou among women

—And blessed is the fruit of thy womb, Jesus.

—Holy Mary

—Mother of God—are so many acts of praise and honor, lovingly addressed to the Blessed Virgin.

All are drawn from Sacred Scripture or the tradition of the Church. And all are so many acts of praise of the Divine Majesty for the gifts bestowed on the one who gave the Son of God his finite humanity.

Invocation builds on veneration. Because Mary is so pleasing to the Trinity, she, more than any other creature, can effectively plead for us before the Throne of God. We invoke her so that she might intercede for us.

The last three parts of the Hail Mary are all forms of invocation:

—Pray for us sinners
—Now
—And at the hour of our death—are confident petitions asking Mary to pray for us on the three levels that we most need supernatural help from the Mother of Divine Grace. We plead for mercy from an offended God: mercy for ourselves and others, mercy of forgiveness of the guilt—or loss of grace—incurred by our sins; mercy of remission of the penalty due to our willful rejection of God's love. We plead for help now, right now, at every conscious moment of our lives to enlighten our minds so we may know what God wants us to do, and help to strengthen our wills so we may do His will. Finally, we plead for the gift of final perseverance to leave this life in divine friendship and enter eternity in the grace of God.

Imitation finally builds on invocation because without help from her Son we could never imitate the virtues of His Mother. Those virtues span the Litany of our Lady. Unlike her Son who possessed the beatific vision from the moment of conception, Mary had to believe and trust. Her faith is to be a model for our acceptance of revealed truth without comprehending why or how. Her hope is the pattern for our trustful confidence that God will see us through this valley of tears to our heavenly home.

But it is especially Mary's charity that we are to strive to follow in our daily lives. Her love for God was the highest of any angel or saint. As His Mother, she loved Him with "love beyond all telling." Yet she never separated this contemplative love of God from the selfless love of others. Her going "in haste" to help her kinswoman Elizabeth, her concern for the wedding guests at Cana because "they have no wine" were only episodes that the gospels briefly touch on to reveal what we know was a lifetime of service to others.

IV.

"SUFFERED UNDER PONTIUS PILATE, WAS CRUCIFIED, DIED, AND WAS BURIED"

We get some idea of the importance of this article of the Creed from St. Paul's statement to the Corinthians, that "I judged not myself to know anything among you, but Jesus Christ, and Him crucified" (I Corinthians 2:2).

Christ's Passion, death, and burial should be deeply understood. They are the crowning proof of God's love for us. They are also the most powerful motive for our loving God, and the model of how we are to love Him in return.

There are four verbs in this article, and each deserves a volume of explanation. Jesus Christ *suffered;* He was *crucified, died,* and was *buried.*

The narrative of Christ's Passion in the gospels amounts to a total of four hundred verses, excluding Christ's five-chapter discourse at the Last Supper, given by St. John. The sheer amount of revealed data indicates the importance of the Redeemer's sufferings, in the mind of the Holy Spirit who inspired the Sacred Scriptures.

Sufferings of Christ

Suffering is the experience of pain. It is the bodily and spiritual experience of what we naturally dislike, the conscious endurance of what we find disagreeable, and the mental awareness that we are undergoing what is against our spontaneous human desires.

Immediately we see that we can react in two opposite ways to a painful experience. We can either resist, or we can patiently endure what we experience. In fact, patience is the willing endurance of pain. Christ's sufferings, we know, were borne with patience. This deserves some explanation and is most clearly seen in the hours of His bloody agony in the Garden of Olives.

He naturally shrank from pain, no less than we do. After all, He was truly human. This becomes evident from the prayer He addressed to His heavenly Father when He begged, "If you are willing, take this chalice from me." But having said this, He promptly added, "Nevertheless let your will be done, not mine." Thereupon, "an angel appeared to Him, coming from heaven, to give Him strength" (Luke 22:42–43).

The first part of Christ's prayer was the expression of His human feelings, the instinctive and involuntary dread of pain. The second part was the manifestation of His patience, the voluntary acceptance of what His natural feelings dreaded. And the appearance of the angel came after He had spoken His resignation to the will of the Father. The angel, be it noted, did not remove the pain but provided Him with additional strength for His will to bear the suffering with patient resignation to the will of God.

So we might go through the whole account of the sufferings of Jesus, from the agony in Gethsemane to the crucifixion on Calvary. Christ's sufferings were always both in the body and in the soul. In the body was the pain caused by emotional reaction to being scourged and crowned with thorns, being forced to carry a heavy cross and then nailed to the Cross and allowed to die by having the body totally drained of its blood.

In the soul was the pain of rejection and humiliation, of opposition by His enemies and abandonment by His friends, of a sense of failure at seeing so many clamoring for His death, who only a few days before were praising Him to the skies, of the cruel ingratitude from the very people for whom He had done so much, even to working numerous miracles in their favor.

To all of this present suffering that Jesus experienced during the hours of His Passion in Palestine, we must add the pain He endured by anticipating the future. Even as man, He foresaw that multitudes in the centuries to come would ignore the sufferings and reject His grace. Yet He bore all of this pain patiently with His human will, while all His instinctive human feelings recoiled at the very thought of so much agony.

The Crucifixion. Among the Jews, no form of death was considered more disgraceful than crucifixion. And among the pagan Romans, no form of execution was considered more painful than to be crucified.

What needs to be stressed is that Christ chose to be crucified. Both on the level of humiliation and of agonizing pain, He chose to undergo crucifixion because he wanted to show His love for us in the extreme. It cannot be emphasized too much that when revelation tells us Jesus chose the Cross, this is no mere symbolism or figure of speech. The Savior had every option possible—either to redeem us without suffering, or to redeem by experiencing pain; again, either to suffer or suffer to the limit of human ingenuity to inflict emotional and physical pain. He chose the outer limits of agony, and did so with perfect freedom.

We say that Christ endured the Cross, and the expression is correct enough. But it does not fully express what actually occurred. It was not only the passive, even the patient endurance of the inevitable: It was the conscious and deliberate choice of what Jesus need not have suffered at all. Yet He decided with His mind and freely chose with His will what He knew was the worst form of pain.

Death of Christ. It may seem strange to profess that Christ was not only crucified, but that He died. What are we saying? We are saying that Jesus redeemed the world from sin by enduring the consequences of sin, which are death.

The sin of our first parents deprived them and their descendants of the supernatural life they possessed before they fell. Already in Genesis, they were told by God that in whatever day they disobeyed Him they would die. Eve was reassured by the devil that God was not telling the truth. She prevailed upon Adam to join her in resisting the divine will.

The inevitable happened. Bodily death entered the world through the devil's instigation, as the visible result of the spiritual death that took place with the first grave offense committed against God by human beings.

When Christ decided to redeem us, He chose the very form of penalty that, as God, He had laid on a sinful human race. His bodily death on Calvary, therefore, was not coincidental: It was deeply providential. It was expiation by God become man by suffering for our sake the price of our redemption.

What occurred when Jesus died? It was the separation of His human soul from His human body. There was no question of Christ's humanity being for a moment separated from the Second Person of the Trinity. Although His body and soul were separated from each other, both remained united with His Divinity. Thus every drop of blood that Jesus shed on Calvary was literally the blood of the living God.

Burial in the Grave. The burial of Christ's body was consistent with His predestined plan of man's redemption, and all four evangelists tell the story of where and how Jesus was buried.

The initiative for burying the Savior came from Joseph of Arimathea, a councillor of high rank and a disciple of Jesus. He went boldly to Pilate to ask for the body. Pilate wondered if Jesus was already dead. So he sent for the centurion who witnessed the crucifixion. "And when he learned from the centurion that He was, he granted the body to Joseph" (Mark 15:45). Joseph then took the body down from the Cross. He wrapped it in a clean linen cloth and laid it in his own new tomb that had been hewn out of the rock. Then he rolled a large stone across the entrance of the tomb. With Joseph at the burial was also Nicodemus, who had first come to Jesus by night for fear of the Jews. Watching the burial were Mary, the mother of Jesus, and Mary Magdalene.

The detailed account of the burial verified that Christ was truly dead: that He was completely wrapped up in a shroud; that His body was placed in a stone tomb; and that the tomb was sealed with a huge rock.

We are further told that the day after the burial, the chief priests and the Pharisees went in a body to Pilate. They told the procurator:

"That deceiver said, while he was yet alive, 'After three days I will rise again.' Give orders, therefore, that the sepulchre be guarded until the third day, or else his disciples may come and steal him away, and say to the people, 'He has risen from the dead'; and the last imposture will be worse than the first." Pilate said to them, "You have a guard; go, guard it as well as you know how." So they went and made the sepulchre secure, sealing the stone and setting the guard (Matthew 27:63–66).

All of these details are priceless evidence that the resurrection of Christ on Easter Sunday was an historical fact.

V.

"He Descended into Hell. On the Third Day, He Rose Again from the Dead"

There are two truths of faith affirmed in this article of the Creed. The first is that after Christ died, His soul—separated from the body—visited the souls of the faithful departed in what has come to be called the Limbo of the Fathers. The second truth is the Resurrection of Christ from the grave on Easter Sunday. While the Resurrection of Christ is far more significant, His descent "into hell" deserves to be better known.

The Descent of Christ

It is not difficult to trace the origins of the statement that, after He died, Jesus "descended into hell." Pre-Christian Judaism is clear on the point. By whatever name it was called, Jewish believers by the time of Christ held that there was an abode of the departed just. It was assumed to be a place or state of happiness, temporary, and was to be replaced by a condition of final or permanent bliss when the Messiah came to establish His kingdom.

On the strength of this tradition, the Apostles' Creed affirms the existence of a limbo—distinct from hell and purgatory—for the just who had died before Christ's ascension into heaven. Because of the Fall, heaven was closed to human beings. In other words, actual possession of the beatific vision was postponed even for those who were purified of all sin. They would enjoy the vision of God only after the Redemption was historically completed by Christ's visible ascension into heaven. This was implied in the Savior's promise to the penitent thief on Calvary. "This day," he was assured, "you will be with me in Paradise" (Luke 24:43).

The reason for Christ's visit to the faithful departed seems evident from the circumstances. He wished to reassure these justified souls that they were, indeed, redeemed and their entrance into heaven was near at hand.

The Resurrection

Christianity as the religion of history and Christ as the living God made man depend on His resurrection from the dead.

We shall therefore examine the Resurrection in a series of questions: What is the Resurrection? Why did Jesus Christ rise from the grave? And how are we to make the Resurrection more meaningful in our lives?

What is the Resurrection? The Resurrection is the historic event of Christ reuniting His human body and soul, which had been separated by His death on Calvary.

Christ had a true human nature, like ours except for sin. Since he had no sin, He need not have died. He chose to die. But by the same free will by which He chose death, He also chose to conquer death and return to the human life He possessed before the first Good Friday.

It was the same Jesus Christ who rose on Easter Sunday. It was the same Divine Person united with His human nature. St. Luke describes the scene on Easter Sunday when the Lord appeared to the eleven disciples as they huddled together in the upper chamber in Jerusalem. They were listening to the two disciples who had just been with Jesus on their way to Emmaus:

Now while they were talking of these things, Jesus stood in their midst, and said to them, "Peace to you! It is I, do not be afraid." But they were startled and panic-stricken, and thought they saw a spirit. And He said to them, "Why are you disturbed, and why do doubts arise in your hearts? See my hands and feet, that it is I myself. Feel me and see; for a spirit does not have flesh and bones, as you see I have." And having said this, He showed them His hands and feet. But as they still disbelieved and marvelled for joy, He said, "Have you anything here to eat?" And they offered Him a piece of broiled fish and a honey-comb. And when He had eaten in their presence He took what remained and gave it to them (Luke 24:36–43).

The apostles were absolutely certain about Christ's bodily resurrection from the dead. This became the foundation of all their preaching. On Pentecost Sunday, Peter told the Jews that the Jesus whom they had crucified had come back to life. And he rested the credibility of the Christian faith on this historical fact.

Why the Resurrection? Christ rose from the dead as the crowning miracle of His visible stay on earth. He worked many miracles during His three years of public ministry: paralytics began to use their limbs, the blind were restored their sight, deaf-mutes could hear and speak; Christ calmed the storm at sea with a single command, He walked on water and gave Peter the power to do the same; the dead were raised from the grave. And not long before His Passion, He called the dead Lazarus out of the tomb.

On this level, His own resurrection was only the culmination of a series of wonders that made Christ's astounding doctrine acceptable by the human mind.

Moreover, by rising from the dead, He proved that He had overcome sin, which was the original cause of death.

Finally, Christ's resurrection is the promise and prelude of our own final resurrection on the last day. He is, as St. Paul tells us, the first fruits of those who sleep. The mystery of death, which we all naturally fear, is balanced by the confident hope that we, too, will rise from the grave.

Our souls are naturally immortal. When they leave the body they remain alive, to enter an eternity whose happiness or misery depends on how well we have served God during our mortal life on earth.

Our bodies will decay and return to the dust from which they come. But only for awhile. In God's own time, provided we have been faithful to the divine will before death, these dead bodies will walk and speak and hear and see again. They will be glorified. This means they will be immortal, never to die again. They will be resplendent with beauty, never again endure pain, and will be able to move through space and matter, not unlike the risen body of Jesus Christ.

The Risen Christ Is Alive. Having become man, the Son of God will always remain man. The expression, "Jesus Christ, yesterday, today, and forever" has been literally verified until now and is prophesied into the endless reaches of eternity.

In the next article of the Creed, we profess to believe in Christ's ascension into heaven. But there would have been no ascension unless there had first been a true bodily resurrection. So, too, when we reflect on the Holy Eucharist, the key to understanding the Real Presence is the fact that God became man, died, and rose from the dead. Why is this the key? Because the Eucharist is the Risen Christ living in our midst in the Blessed Sacrament.

VI.

"He Ascended into Heaven, and Is Seated at the Right Hand of God, the Father Almighty"

Jesus Christ arose from the dead and remained upon earth in visible form for forty days. On the fortieth day, He ascended into heaven. As described by St. Luke, Jesus had just finished telling His disciples they would receive the power of the Holy Spirit:

> When He had said these things, while they looked on, He was raised up. And a cloud received Him out of their sight. And while they were beholding Him going up to heaven, behold two men stood by them in white garments. They said, "You men of Galilee, why do you stand looking up to heaven? This Jesus who is taken up from you into heaven will come as you have seen Him going up to heaven" (Acts 1:9–11).

Christ's ascension into heaven was a historical event. He actually did leave the earth and was physically seen to ascend into the heavens. However, the "heavens" to which he went were not the "corporeal heavens" of sun, moon, and stars. When St. Paul says that "He ascended above the heavens" (Ephesians 4:10), this meant not only above the stellar regions but even above all "spiritual heavens." Christ's place in heaven is above all the angels and saints. He ascended even to the Throne of God the Father. He is now at the Father's "right hand in the heavenly places. He is above all principality and power, and virtue and dominion, and every name that is named not only in this world but also in that which is to come" (Ephesians 1:20–21).

The expression "right hand" is not to be taken literally but symbolically, when we speak of God. Christ as God is said to sit at the right hand of the Father because He is equal with the Father. As man, He is seated at the Father's "right hand" as being closest to God in the possession of the highest perfection possible for a created nature. This is what the devil craved when he said, "I will ascend into heaven. I will exalt my throne above the stars . . . I will be like the most high" (Isaiah 14:13–14). But Christ alone rose to that height. This is what He meant when He applied to Himself the messianic prophecy of David: "The Lord said to my Lord: 'Sit at my right hand' " (Psalm 109:1).

Why the Ascension? The Church tells us that Christ ascended into heaven, because heaven was due to Him according to His Divine nature. It is natural for something to return to the place of its origin. Christ drew His origin from God who is above all. No doubt the saints are also in heaven, but they did not reach there as Christ did. He ascended by His own power, whereas the saints are taken to heaven by the power of Christ.

Moreover, heaven was due to Christ as the fruit of His victory. He was sent by the Father into the world in order to overcome the devil, and He overcame the prince of this world. That is why He merited to be exalted above all things, and promises us a share in His exaltation, provided that like Him—and with His grace—we too overcome the evil spirit. "To him that shall overcome," He tells us, "I will give to sit with me on my throne; as also I have overcome, and am set down with my Father on His throne" (Revelation 3:21).

Finally, Christ's ascension was the reward of His humility. Since there was no one more humble than Christ, He deserved to be more elevated than anyone else. Although He was God, He chose to become man. And though He was the Lord of all, He chose to become a servant and become obedient unto death, even to death on the Cross. He therefore merited to be raised to the heights of heaven. Why? Because humility is the road to exaltation.

Lessons of the Ascension. Every mystery of the faith is meant to teach us something. The Ascension is no exception.

Because of Christ's ascension, our faith in Him as our Leader and Guide is strengthened. During His mortal stay on earth He taught us how we should live, so that, like Him, we too might reach heaven. He told us, "I go to prepare a place for you" (John 14:2). We shall see Him in heavenly glory provided we have been willing to suffer like Him, even in rejection and being ignored.

Our Lord's ascension should strengthen our trust in His power of interceding for us with the eternal Father. This is what we mean by Christ's everlasting priesthood, "whereby He is able to save forever those who come to God by Him. He is always living to make intercession for us" (Hebrews 7:25).

The Ascension of Christ is a powerful motive for loving Him. We were made by God out of nothing, but we are destined to possess the Living God in our human, bodily form, if only we learn to despise temporal things. St. Paul warns us: "If you be risen with Christ, seek the things that are above, where Christ is sitting at the right hand of God. Mind the things that are above, not the things that are upon the earth" (Colossians 3:1–2). The cost of giving up earthly pleasures may seem to be high. But it is more than worth the effort as we look up to Christ waiting for us to join Him in our eternal home.

VII.

"From Thence He Shall Come to Judge the Living and the Dead"

There is only one final judge of the human race. It is God by whom the world was first created and to whom we are destined in eternity to return. What may be less obvious is that this same Almighty God became man in the person of Christ. Consequently, Jesus Christ has the divine right to judge all mankind.

Immediately we distinguish between the Lord judging us individually at the moment of death, and judging us as the human family at the end of the world. We call the first judgment particular and the second general. They are not the same.

Particular Judgment

The individual judgment of each person at death will be made by Jesus Christ. As understood by the Church, right after death the eternal destiny of each separate soul is decided by the just judgment of God. Those leaving the body in the state of grace, but in need of purification, are cleansed in purgatory. Souls that are perfectly pure are at once admitted to the beatific vision of the Holy Trinity. Those who depart in actual mortal sin are at once sent to eternal punishment, whose intensity depends on the gravity of their sin.

The biblical evidence for the particular judgment is mainly indirect. While no single passage in the Bible explicitly affirms this dogma, there are several that teach an immediate retribution after death. Therefore the particular judgment is clearly implied in Sacred Scripture.

Thus Christ represents Lazarus and the rich man (Dives) as receiving their respective reward and punishment immediately after death. To the penitent thief on Calvary, Jesus promised that his soul, instantly on leaving the body, would be in the state of the blessed: "This day, you will be with me in Paradise" (Luke 23:43). St. Paul longs to be absent from the body that he may be present with the Lord, clearly understanding death to be the entrance into his reward (Philippians 1:21–23). The Old Testament speaks of a retribution at the hour of death (Ecclesiasticus 11:28–29).

This is also the understanding of the great Fathers of the Church, like St. Augustine and St. Ephraem. They spoke of two "second comings of Christ." The first is when we die, and the second on the last day of the whole human race. As the earliest acts of the martyrs and liturgies reveal, the martyrs were persuaded of the prompt reward of their loyalty to Christ. This belief is shown in the ancient practice of honoring and invoking the saints, even those who were not martyrs. The Church's practice of canonizing the saints simply confirms the traditional belief that we shall all be judged on our final destiny the moment we leave time and enter eternity.

General Judgment

Few truths are more frequently or more clearly proclaimed in the Scriptures than the fact of a general judgment.

The Old Testament prophets refer to this judgment in speaking of "The Day of the Lord" (Joel 2:31; Isaiah 2:12), when all the nations will be summoned to be judged by the Lord of all.

In the New Testament, the Second Coming (*Parousia*) of Christ as Judge of the World is woven into the whole mystery of salvation. The Lord's prediction of the Last Day covers the whole twenty-fifth chapter of the Gospel of St. Matthew as an appropriate introduction to the long narrative of Christ's Passion in Chapter twenty-six.

Story of the Two Parables. Chapter twenty-five opens with two parables about the five foolish and the five wise virgins, and about the master who goes on a journey and leaves three of his servants with varying amounts of money to put to good use in his absence. In the first parable, the five foolish virgins fail to bring enough oil for their lamps to meet the bridegroom (Christ). By the time they reach the marriage feast "the door was shut." The bridegroom tells them, "I do not know you." Then Christ's warning to all of us: "Watch, therefore, because you know not the day nor the hour" (Matthew 25:1–13).

In the second parable, when the master (Christ) returns from his journey he demands an account of his servants. The servants who received five and two talents respectively wisely put their talents to good use and earned another five and two talents each as a result. They were both praised by the master and handsomely rewarded. But the man who had been given only one talent buried it and apologized for his neglect. He was cast out into the exterior darkness. There shall be weeping and gnashing of teeth.

Prediction of the Last Day. Anticipating His prophecy of the general judgment, Christ foretold the destruction of Jerusalem (Matthew 24:1–51). The logic of His prediction is clear. Since no less than Jerusalem itself was actually destroyed as Christ had predicted, so the final judgment of mankind will certainly take place.

What is most instructive is the detail of Christ's teaching about who and how the world will be judged: "When the Son of Man shall come in His majesty, and all the angels with Him, then shall He sit upon the seat of His majesty."

Who shall be judged? "All nations shall be gathered together before Him. And He shall separate them one from another, as the shepherd separates the sheep from the goats. And He shall set the sheep on His right hand, but the goats on His left."

How shall we be judged? On the basis of our practice of selfless charity:

> Then shall the king say to them on His right hand, "Come, blessed of my Father, possess the Kingdom prepared for you from the foundation of the world. For I was hungry and you gave me to eat. I was thirsty, and you gave me to drink. I was a stranger and you took me in; naked, and you covered me; sick, and you visited me. I was in prison and you came to me" (Matthew 25:34–36).

The saved will then ask Christ when did they minister to His needs, and He will tell them, "As long as you did it to one of these, my least brethren, you did it to me."

Then will follow the same dialogue with those who are lost. They will be told, "Depart from me you cursed, into everlasting fire which was prepared for the devil and his angels." They will be condemned on the same grounds as the first will be saved. "As long as you did it not to one of these least, neither did you do it to me."

The prophecy of the general judgment closes with one of the single most important verses in the Bible. Christ foretells that those who failed in charity "shall go into everlasting punishment," but those who had selflessly met the needs of others, "the just," shall go "into life everlasting" (Matthew 25:31–46).

He uses the same identical word, "everlasting," in Greek *aionios,* to describe the endless pains of hell as well as the endless joys of heaven.

VIII.

"I Believe in the Holy Spirit"

The best way to understand what we mean by our profession of faith in the Holy Spirit is to compare it with our faith in the Son of God. In God there is intellect and will, corresponding to thinking and loving in human beings. Scripture identifies the mind of God with the Word of God, as St. John tells us: "In the beginning was the Word, and the Word was with God, and the Word was God" (John 1:1). "So, just as the Word of God is the Son of God, so the Love of God is the Holy Spirit" (St. Thomas Aquinas. *Exposition of the Apostles' Creed,* Article 8).

That is why we can say that a person has the Holy Spirit when he loves God. St. Paul tells us that, "The charity of God is poured forth in our hearts by the Holy Spirit who is given to us" (Romans 5:5).

Over the centuries there were those who had the erroneous idea that the Holy Spirit is a mere creature. They believed He is less than the Father and the Son; in fact, that He is God's servant and minister. That is why from earliest times the Church added no less than five articles to the Creed about the Holy Spirit.

Given the importance of this subject, it is worth comparing the Holy Spirit with the different kinds of created spirits that we believe exist in the world, and see how the Holy Spirit is unique as the Third Person of the Holy Trinity.

There are first of all created spirits that are angels. They are "all ministering spirits" (Hebrews 1:4). But the Holy Spirit is not the created spirit of the angels: The Holy Spirit is Divine. John tells us "God is a Spirit" (John 2:24), and St. Paul says that "The Lord is a Spirit" (II Corinthians 3:17). That is why when the Holy Spirit is given to us, we are able to love God so freely as to sacrifice voluntarily the selfish love of the world: "Where the Spirit of the Lord is, there is liberty" (II Corinthians 3:17). Our faith in the Holy Spirit is our belief that God, who is Love, can share with us something of His own divine love.

There are also the created spirits that are human souls. Our souls give natural life to our bodies. They are immediately created by God out of nothing at the moment of our conception, and infused into our bodies from the first moment of our human existence in our mother's womb. But just as these created spirits give natural life to our bodies, the Holy Spirit conferred at baptism gives supernatural life to our souls. The Holy Spirit is the Uncreated Grace whose indwelling in our souls gives us sanctifying grace, which the Church allows us to call the soul of the soul. The Third Person who dwells in our souls is the Lifegiver whom Christ said would abide in us, provided we believed in the Savior's words (John 6:63).

If we ask, who exactly is the Holy Spirit? we must

say He is one in substance with the Father and the Son. No less than the Son is the Wisdom or the Word of God, so the Holy Spirit is the Love of the Father and the Son. He therefore proceeds from both. Even as God's Wisdom is of one substance with the Father, so God's Love is one in substance with the Father and the Son. In the Nicene Creed we say, "We believe in the Holy Spirit, the Lord, the giver of life; *He proceeds from the Father and the Son.*" The closing phrase, "and the Son" in Latin reads *Filioque,* and has made doctrinal history. It was inserted with papal approval to counteract the heresy that claimed the Holy Spirit proceeds only from the Father. Since the thirteenth century, the *Filioque* has been one of the chief grounds of opposition by the Eastern Orthodox Church to the Church of Rome.

Given the perfect equality of the Holy Spirit with the Father and the Son, He is to be equally worshipped with the First and Second Persons of the Trinity. That is why St. John declares that "true adorers shall adore the Father in Spirit and in Truth" (John 4:23). That is also why Christ told His disciples to "teach all nations, baptizing them in the name of the Father, and of the Son, and of the Holy Spirit" (Matthew 28:19). The three Persons of the Trinity have only one Divine Name, since they have only one Divine nature. Finally, that is why the Nicene Creed adds the statement about the Holy Spirit, "who together with the Father and the Son is equally adored and glorified."

Sacred Scriptures teach us that the Holy Spirit is equal to God. We know that the ancient prophets spoke on behalf of God. St. Peter tells us that, "The holy men of God spoke inspired by the Holy Spirit" (II Peter 1:21). That is why the Nicene Creed also adds the sentence, "He spoke through the prophets," referring to the Holy Spirit. Again, in reprimanding Ananias for deceitfully withholding some of his property from the Christian community, Peter asked him, "How can Satan have so possessed you that you should lie to the Holy Spirit? . . . It is not to men than you have lied, but to God" (Acts 5:3, 5).

Our Catholic religion is filled with professions of faith in the influence of the Holy Spirit in our lives. We speak of the gifts of the Holy Spirit as the supernatural instincts or impulses that urge us to put the virtues of faith, hope, and charity into practice. We have the fruits of the Holy Spirit that give us a deep supernatural satisfaction in doing the will of God. But more specifically, the Church identifies certain ways in which the Holy Spirit enters our lives.

He cleanses our souls from sin. This follows logically from the fact that the same One by whom our souls were created is the One by whom they are to be repaired. Since it was through the love of God that human souls were made, this same Love, who is the Holy Spirit, must restore souls to His divine friendship.

The Holy Spirit enlightens our minds. Whatever we know by faith, we have received by the power of the Spirit. This is what Christ meant when He promised the "the Holy Spirit, the Paraclete [Advocate] whom the Father will send in my name, will Himself teach you all things and will bring all things to your mind, whatsoever I shall have said to you" (John 14:26). Christ was the first Advocate who revealed the mysteries of God. The Holy Spirit is the second Advocate who enables us to understand what Christ had revealed.

The Holy Spirit enables us by His grace to observe the divine commandments. As God foretold in the Old Testament: "I will put my Spirit in the midst of you. I will cause you to walk in my commandments and to keep my judgments and do them" (Ezekiel 36:27). Except for the power of the Holy Spirit, sent by Christ, we could not live up to the humanly impossible demands of the Savior on His followers.

On Pentecost Sunday, the Holy Spirit came down on the apostles in the form of fiery tongues. This was a visible sign of what they were receiving interiorly, namely, light to accept the teaching of Jesus, and the strength to witness to Him even at the price of their blood.

IX.

"The Holy Catholic Church: the Communion of Saints"

Having professed our faith in the Holy Spirit, we continue by professing to believe in the Holy Catholic Church, of which the Holy Spirit is the soul or source of her corporate life.

In one sense, the Church began with the origins of the human race. God wants to save people not only as individuals but as members of society. Consequently the Church corresponds on the level of grace to our social existence on the level of nature.

The foreshadowing of the Church goes back to the call of Abraham, the father of all the faithful. But the Church actually came into existence only with the Incarnation. Here we can find three stages in her establishment. Christ began building the Mystical Body, which is the Church, when by His preaching He made known His precepts to the world. He completed the Church when He died on the Cross. And He proclaimed the Church when He sent the Holy Spirit on the apostles on Pentecost Sunday.

What exactly do we mean when we say that the Church was born on Calvary? We mean that by His death on the Cross, Christ merited the graces that a sinful world needed to be reconciled with an offended God. However, that was only the beginning. Certainly Jesus won for us all the graces that we need to be saved and sanctified. But these graces have to be communicated to the world. It is through the Church, which came into existence on Good Friday, that the Savior ever since has been channeling His grace to the human family. Having founded the Church, Christ made sure she would endure until the end of time. "I am with you," He promised, "all days even to the consummation of the world."

By the close of the apostolic age, the Church's leaders had to take a stand and declare who belongs to her. There was no choice. There were dissenters from within, and opponents from without. By the end of the fourth century, the description of the Church as holy and Catholic was expanded to what we profess in the Nicene Creed: "We believe in one, holy, Catholic, and apostolic Church." These four adjectives have become the four marks that identify the true Church of Christ.

One

The unity of the true Church is a unity of faith and communion. By their union of faith, those who belong to the Church believe the same faith as proposed to them by the Church. By their unity of communion, the faithful submit to the authority of the bishops united with the Bishop of Rome.

We should distinguish, however, between belonging to the Church, and being a member of the Church. Strictly speaking, only those who fully accept all that the Church declares as revealed truth are members of the Catholic Church. Those who are baptized and in varying degrees accept some of the Church's prescribed teachings are said to belong to the Church.

This is clearly brought out in the statement of the Second Vatican Council when it defined the Church founded by Christ and identified her presence in the world today. According to the Council:

> This Church, constituted and organized in the world as a society, *subsists* in the Catholic Church, which is governed by the successor of Peter and the bishops in communion with him. Nevertheless, there are many elements of sanctification and truth found outside her structure. These elements, as gifts belonging to the Church of Christ, are forces impelling toward Catholic unity (*Constitution on the Church*, I, 8).

The important word in this declaration is the verb *subsists*. Behind this carefully chosen word stands the claim that the actual fullness of Christ's heritage to His Church—the fullness of His revealed truth, the fullness of the sacraments He instituted, the fullness of authority to govern the People of God in His name—resides in the Catholic Church of which the Bishop of Rome is the visible head.

Other Christian bodies share, in greater or less

degree, in these elements of sanctification and truth that exist in their divinely intended fullness—hence subsist—in the Roman Catholic Church. These elements, we are told, "are forces impelling toward Catholic unity." In other words, Christian bodies are drawing closer to the unity willed by the Redeemer in the measure that they share in the supernatural riches of the Catholic Church.

Holy

Already in apostolic times, the Church was considered holy. If we inquire more closely in what sense the Church is holy, we find that she is holy three times over: in her purpose for existence; in the means she provides for making people holy; and in the proved holiness of her members.

Why Christ Founded the Church. There is no question that Christ instituted the Church to make her holy. St. Paul told the early Christians to imitate Christ, who "loved the Church and sacrificed Himself for her to make her holy" (Ephesians 5:25).

All of the Savior's preaching and all His exhortations to the disciples had one principal aim: that those who believe in Him would become perfect, even as their heavenly Father is perfect. Christ not only preached holiness, but He practiced it to a sublime degree and then told His followers to follow His example. Moreover, He sent them His Holy Spirit to move everyone interiorly to love God with their whole heart, and to love one another as He had loved them.

How the Church Sanctifies. Having founded the Church to sanctify her members, Christ provided teachings of faith and morals: the Sacrifice of the Mass and the sacraments, especially the Eucharist; the directives of ecclesiastical authority; and especially His indwelling Holy Spirit.

One other means of sanctification is available but it must be used to be efficacious, namely the free will of those who belong to the Church. There is no substitute for the willingness to listen to the Church's teaching, to obey her directives, and to make use of the sacraments on the road to sanctity.

What Are the Fruits of Sanctity? Two thousand years of history show how effective the Church of Christ is in producing holiness.

Already in the first century, St. Paul addressed the Christians as "saints." He called individual communities as well as the whole Church, "the Church of God" (I Corinthians 1:2). Since the days of the catacombs, members of the Church have given evidence of above-ordinary holiness. Martyrs and confessors of the faith; men, women, and even children; persons of every social level; the rich and the poor—the Church's history is the story of countless believers who practiced exalted virtue because they had access to extraordinary sources of divine grace in the Catholic Church.

Catholic

The word "Catholic" means "universal." As a title for the Church, it was first used by St. Ignatius of Antioch in 107 A.D. when he wrote, "Where Jesus Christ is, there is the Catholic Church." The term soon acquired the two meanings that are now associated with "Catholic," namely *universal* and *orthodox*.

Christ certainly intended His Church to be universal, when He told His disciples: "All authority in heaven and on earth has been given to me. Go, therefore, make disciples of all nations" (Matthew 28:18–19). We get some idea of how well the apostles obeyed Christ's command from the fact that there were some one hundred Catholic dioceses established in Europe, Asia, and Africa by the beginning of the second century.

The Church's universality had to be joined with her orthodoxy to ensure true catholicity. This would have been impossible except for her final quality of being truly apostolic.

Apostolic

The Church is apostolic on several grounds: her origin, doctrine, authority, and episcopal succession.

- She is apostolic because her origin reaches back to Christ's call of the apostles and ordaining them to the fullness of the priesthood at the Last Supper.

- She is also apostolic because the doctrine she has taught over the centuries has remained faithful to the teaching of the apostles.

- She is apostolic because the pope's and bishops' authority to teach, govern, and sanctify comes from their being direct successors of St. Peter and the first apostles.

- She is finally apostolic because this succession derives not only by delegation or appointment, but is actually rooted in episcopal ordination. When Christ ordained the apostles, He enabled them to confer the same powers they had received from Him. And the bishops ordained by the apostles could transmit their episcopal powers—in unending line—to their successors until the end of time.

Papal Primacy.   The Bishop of Rome is the successor of the Apostle Peter. Christ promised Peter that He would make him the rock on which He would build His Church (Matthew 16:18). After the Resurrection, Christ actually gave Peter the authority to teach and govern the universal Church. Peter was told to "feed my lambs" and "feed my sheep" by nourishing their minds with Christ's truth, and to "tend my sheep" by leading the wills of the faithful according to the will of Christ.

The popes as Bishops of Rome have succeeded St. Peter as visible heads of the Church on earth.

From the first centuries they have been thus recognized by all believing Catholics. The pope is therefore called the Vicar of Christ because he has received from the Divine Master delegated authority over all the People of God.

His authority is called the papal primacy. It means that he has supreme authority to teach and govern the universal Church. This authority is not merely nominal, but real: It is not merely honorary, but binding in conscience on everyone who belongs to the Catholic Church.

Episcopal Collegiality. From earliest times, the apostles and then their successors worked together collectively. They cooperated with one another, under the Bishop of Rome, in what we now call episcopal collegiality.

As stated by the Second Vatican Council: "St. Peter and the other apostles constitute a single apostolic college. In like manner, the Roman Pontiff, Peter's successor, and the bishops, successors of the apostles are linked together" (*Dogmatic Constitution on the Church*, III, 22). In further commenting on collegiality, the council carefully explained the relationship between the bishops and the pope.

There are three basic powers that belong to the episcopacy:

- First is the power of administering the sacraments, including the consecration of other men as bishops.

- Second is the power of teaching authoritatively and sharing in the Church's guidance by the Holy Spirit to communicate revealed truth.

- Third is the right to govern and direct the faithful according to the norms of worship and conduct that are binding on all the People of God.

Among these three powers, the first comes to a bishop when he is consecrated. He should not, however, exercise this power without the pope's approval. But if he does, he acts validly. The sacraments he confers—including the ordination of other bishops—produce their effect as soon as the sacrament is received.

The second and third powers of a bishop are quite different. They are, of course, rooted in the bishop's consecration. But this consecration gives a bishop only the capacity to teach and govern, not the actual power of doing so. As interpreted by the Vatican Council, "episcopal consecration confers the offices of teaching and ruling." This, however, is not enough. "Of their nature they *can only* be exercised in hierarchical communion with the head and members of the college."

What are we being told? Episcopal collegiality becomes effective only if a bishop, or group of bishops, is in actual communion with Rome and the rest of the hierarchy united with the pope. Apart from such communion, any episcopal action has no assurance of divine approval, no matter how many prelates may agree among themselves.

Infallibility. One of the consequences of the Church's being apostolic is that she must necessarily be infallible in teaching the essentials of faith and morals. Otherwise, Christ would have left her in open contradiction. On the one hand He obliged His followers to accept the teaching of Peter and the apostles as a necessary condition for salvation. On the other hand, He would not have assured His Church of proclaiming the truth, which alone deserves to be accepted and followed, if He had not endowed her with infallibility.

He told the apostles: "If anyone does not . . . listen to what you have to say, as you walk out of the house or town shake the dust from your feet. I tell you solemnly, on the day of Judgment it will not go as hard with the land of Sodom and Gomorrah as with that town" (Matthew 10:14–15). Later on, he told Peter: "I will give you the keys of the kingdom of heaven. Whatever you bind on earth shall be considered bound in heaven. Whatever you loose on earth shall be considered loosed in heaven" (Matthew 16:19).

Infallibility is preservation from error. Properly speaking, only persons can be infallible. When they teach infallibly, their teaching may also be said to be infallible, although more accurately it is irreversible. What has once been taught infallibly cannot be substantially changed or reversed. Truth is essentially unchangeable.

The primary source of infallible teaching is the successor of St. Peter, when he intends to bind the consciences of all believers in matters of faith or morals. What he thus teaches is irreversible because of its very nature and not because others in the Church agree with him. This was solemnly defined by the First Vatican Council.

At the Second Vatican Council, the doctrine of infallibility was further refined. Individual bishops, the council declared, are not infallible:

> Yet, when, in the course of their authentic teaching on faith or morals, they agree on one position to be held as definitive, they are proclaiming infallibly the teaching of Christ. This happens when, though scattered throughout the world, they observe the bond of fellowship tying them to each other and to Peter's successor (*Constitution on the Church,* III, 25).

In other words, the Holy Spirit guides the successors of the apostles as teachers of the truth, provided they are united among themselves and under the Bishop of Rome.

Communion of Saints. The Church founded by Christ has three levels of existence. She is the Church Militant on earth, the Church Suffering in purgatory, and the Church Triumphant in heaven. After the last day, there will be only the Church Triumphant in heavenly glory.

It is understood that there is communication

among these three levels of the Mystical Body. Those on earth invoke the saints in heaven and pray for the souls in purgatory. Those in heaven pray for the Church Militant and the Church Suffering; they obtain graces for us on earth and an alleviation of suffering for the poor souls. Those in purgatory can invoke the saints on high and pray for us struggling with the world, the flesh, and the evil spirit.

We might, then, describe the Communion of Saints as the unity and cooperation of the whole Church. Together, we all form one Mystical Body. We share our merits and prayers with one another for the greater glory of God and the upbuilding of Christ's Body which is His Church.

X.

"THE FORGIVENESS OF SINS"

It is deeply significant that the Apostles' Creed affirms our belief in the forgiveness of sins immediately after professing our faith in the holy Catholic Church. These two mysteries belong together.

On Easter Sunday, Jesus told the two saddened disciples on the way to Emmaus: "You see how it is written that the Christ would suffer and on the third day rise from the dead, and that in His name repentance for the forgiveness of sins would be preached to all the nations beginning from Jerusalem" (Luke 24:46–47).

What was the Savior saying? He was not only predicting that the gospel would be preached to all nations. He foretold that sins would be forgiven to those who repented.

The key element in this article of the Creed is that the Church founded by Christ actually has the power to forgive sins in His name. We therefore not only believe that God is merciful, nor only that He forgives those who repent of their wrongdoing. We believe that Christ entrusted His Church with a share in His own divine power to remove the guilt and the penalty due to sins, no less than He had done personally during His public ministry in Palestine.

The heart of Catholic Christianity is in the preceding statement. We believe that the same Jesus who told the paralytic, "Courage, son, your sins are forgiven," and told the sinful woman in the house of Simon the Pharisee, "Your sins are forgiven" (Matthew 9:2; Luke 7:48), continues His mission of healing souls through the Church that He founded.

It is not only that God's mercy is to be proclaimed, but He literally remits sin by the ministry of the Church now on earth. Thus sins are remitted by the sacrament of baptism, as witnessed on Pentecost Sunday. And sins after baptism are also remitted by what the Church calls "the power of the keys." This power is not possessed by all Christians, but only by those who have been ordained to the priesthood. This has always been the Church's understanding of Christ's words on Easter Sunday night when Christ told the apostles: "Receive the Holy Spirit. For those whose sins you forgive, they are forgiven; for those whose sin you retain, they are retained" (John 20:22–23).

Claiming that no one but God can forgive sins, the Pharisees objected when Christ told the paralyzed man, who was lowered in front of Him, "Son, your sins are forgiven you" (Mark 2:5). But God can share this power with human beings.

It is this sharing in the divine power of forgiving sins that the Church believes she possesses. It is the greatest gift that the merciful Christ bequeathed to a sinful world until the end of time.

XI.

"THE RESURRECTION OF THE BODY"

We not only believe that the human soul is immortal, but that the human body is destined to rise immortal from the grave. Unlike our souls, which as spiritual substances are naturally immortal, our bodies are mortal by nature. They were not created subject to death, according to God's original plan for mankind. But the sin of our first parents deprived them and their descendants of the gift of bodily immortality. All of us must die because we are all sinners.

One of the great benefits of Christianity to human wisdom is its clear teaching about both spiritual and bodily immortality.

In the Old Testament, the clearest revelation about the immortality of the soul is found in the Book of Wisdom. We are told:

The souls of the virtuous are in the hands of God, no torment shall ever touch them. In the eyes of the unwise, they did appear to die, their going looked like a disaster, their leaving us like annihilation; but they are in peace. If they experienced punishment as men see it, their hope was rich with immortality; slight was their affliction, great will their blessing be (Wisdom 3:1–4).

The New Testament simply confirms the teaching of the Old on the immortality of the soul. Our Lord could not have been more clear than when He told us, "Do not be afraid of those who kill the body but cannot kill the soul; fear him rather who can destroy both body and soul in hell" (Matthew 10:28).

When the Apostles' Creed was formulated, no explicit mention was made of the soul. But this omission was intended to guard against any idea that the soul dies and is raised up again with the body. One other reason for speaking only of the resurrection of the body was to refute the first-century heresy of Hymeneus and Philetus. They claimed that biblical references to the resurrection are not concerned with the body, but only with the soul's rising from the death of sin to the life of grace.

What we have in the Creed, therefore, is a profession of belief in the real resurrection of the body.

Evidence of Scripture

Already in the Old Testament, Job differed with his "friends" who told him to admit his sinfulness as the cause of his misery. No, Job replied, the real reason for his suffering was the mystery of a just God whom he reluctantly calls "My Oppressor." Then Job declares, "I know that my Redeemer lives, and on the last day I shall rise out of the earth, and I shall be clothed again with my skin, and in my flesh I shall see my God" (Job 19:25–26).

Christ's raising several people from the dead shows that God is willing to have the human body reunited with the soul. And His own resurrection on Easter Sunday is the crowning proof that we, too, are destined by His power to rise one day from the grave.

On two dramatic occasions, Christ foretold that He would raise the dead back to life. When promising the Holy Eucharist, Jesus declared that, "Anyone who does eat my flesh and drink my blood has eternal life, and I shall raise him up on the last day" (John 6:54). Before raising Lazarus, Martha complained to Jesus, "If you had been here, my brother would not have died." The Savior assured her, "Your brother will rise again." To which Martha replied, "I know he will rise again at the resurrection on the last day." Then Jesus said: "I am the resurrection. If anyone believes in me, even though he dies, he will live" (John 11:21, 23–25).

The longest and most explicit teaching in Scripture on the bodily resurrection is in St. Paul's first letter to the Corinthians. The entire fifteenth chapter of fifty-eight verses is on the final resurrection of the body on the last day. It is the climax to the apostle's discourse on the practice of selfless love, which is to be rewarded in eternity, not only in the soul but also in the body.

The Resurrection Is Reasonable

Our bodily resurrection is certainly known by faith: It is part of God's revelation to the human race. Nevertheless, it is also consistent with human reason. St. Paul makes a comparison with what we know in nature. "Whatever you sow in the ground," he explains, "has to die before it is given new life. And the thing that you sow is not what is going to come. You sow a bare grain, say of wheat or something like that, and then God gives it the sort of body that He has chosen. Each sort of seed gets its own sort of body" (I Corinthians 15:37–38). Something like this takes place when our body dies. It is, as it were, sown in the ground. Then, in God's own time, He will raise up from this buried seed the risen body of our glorified humanity.

The early Fathers of the Church dwell at length on these comparisons. The sun, they say, is withdrawn every day from our eyes, as if by dying, and is revealed again, as it were, by rising again. Trees lose their leaves and again, as it were, by a resurrection, regain them. Seeds die by decay and rise again by germination.

But there is more here than merely comparisons with nature. Our souls are immortal. They have a natural tendency to be united to the body. Their permanent separation from the body would be contrary to our human nature. It seems only proper, therefore, that our souls should be rejoined with our bodies.

The Savior Himself appealed to this argument in His conversation with the Sadducees who denied the resurrection of the body (Matthew 22:23–33).

There is further logic in our faith in the resurrection of the body. During life on earth, we serve God not only in our souls but also in our bodies. It is only right that our reward in eternity should be not only spiritual but also bodily. No wonder St. Paul says that, "If for this life only we have hoped in Christ, we are of all men most to be pitied" (I Corinthians 15:19). What the apostle means here is that *even if* the soul could rise without the body, it would still enjoy happiness in the next life. But his exclamation must refer to the whole man. Why? Because unless the body receives the rewards for its earthly labors, those who have endured so many trials and affliction —in body and soul—would indeed be "of all men most to be pitied."

Finally, we are not angels, but human beings. We form one whole, body and soul. The soul cannot be perfectly happy unless the whole of us, body and soul, enjoys the rewards that God has promised to those who love Him.

All Human Beings Will Rise Again

Although the stress in Scripture is on the resurrection of the just, faith tells us that all human beings, the just and the unjust, will rise from their graves. St. Paul's all-inclusive language is plain. "As in Adam," he says, "all die, so also in Christ shall all be made alive" (I Corinthians 15:22). Of course, the condition of all who rise will not be the same. In one of the most formal prophecies He ever made, Christ foretells why and how He will judge the whole human race on the last day.

> I tell you most solemnly the hour will come— in fact it is here already—when the dead will hear the voice of the Son of God, and all who hear it will live. For the Father, who is the source of life, has made the Son the source of life; and because He is the Son of Man has appointed Him supreme judge. Do not be surprised at this, for the hour is coming when the dead will leave their graves at the sound of His voice. Those who did good will rise again to life; those who did evil to condemnation (John 5:25–29).

Divine revelation further teaches about two classes of people who will rise on the last day: those who will have died over the previous centuries, and those who will be alive on the Day of Judgment. The latter will first die and then they, too, will rise from the dead with the rest of the human race (I Thessalonians 4:16–17).

Each Person Will Receive His Own Body

All the evidence of Scripture in the Old and New Testaments indicates that each of us will be reunited with our own individual body. The prophet Job looked forward to the day when, "In my own flesh I shall see God . . . my eyes shall behold Him" (Job 19:26–27). St. Paul reminds us that, "This perishable nature must put on the imperishable" (I Corinthians 15:53).

This stands to reason. It is inconceivable that at the resurrection we would not be essentially the same persons we have been during our mortal lives on earth. As persons, we possess our own body and soul. During the temporary separation of soul from body, each still belongs to each of us as distinct human beings. When our bodies are reunited with our souls, they will be *our* bodies, not someone else's. They will be *our bodies* and not some new creation that never existed before.

All of this is consistent with the whole tenor of divine revelation. It is the individual person, each with his own unique body united with his own unique soul, who will rise on the last day to receive the just recompense for his individual human conduct, in body and soul, during his mortal stay on earth.

Qualities of the Risen Body

We may begin our reflections on the qualities of the risen body with St. Paul.

The basic quality of the risen body will be its immortality. Following the example of Christ, who is "the first fruits of all who have fallen asleep," and by His power and grace, "so all men will be brought to life in Christ. But all of them in their proper order. Christ as the first fruits, and then, after the coming of Christ, those who belong to Him" (I Corinthians 15:20, 22–23). Consequently, "The last enemy to be destroyed is death," so that "Death shall be no more" (I Corinthians 15:26; Revelation 21:4). Note that the wicked will also rise immortal. However, condemned to everlasting suffering, they "will seek death and will not find it; they will long to die, and death will fly from them" (Revelation 9:6). Bodily immortality, then, will be the common inheritance of both the saved and the lost.

Special Qualities of the Glorified Body. St. Paul identifies four distinctive qualities of the risen bodies of the blessed:

> The thing that is sown is perishable, but what is raised is imperishable. The thing that is sown is contemptible, but what is raised is glorious. The thing that is sown is weak, but what is raised is powerful. When it is sown it embodies the soul, when it is raised it embodies the spirit (I Corinthians 15:42–44).

Since the first century, the Church has developed this revealed doctrine about the qualities of the risen bodies of the just. These qualities have been given technical names: impassibility, brightness, agility, and subtility. Each deserves some explanation.

Impassibility means that the risen body will no longer be subject to pain, or even inconvenience of

101

any kind. Piercing cold will not affect the glorified body, nor will the glaring intensity of heat, nor can anything like the forces of nature hurt it. Since there will be no more death, neither will there be the earthly prelude to death, which is sickness and disease.

Brightness describes that property of the glorified bodies that will make them shine like the sun. In Christ's own words, "Then the virtuous will shine like the sun in the kingdom of the Father" (Matthew 13:43). The Savior briefly manifested what this brightness is like in His transfiguration on "a high mountain." There in the presence of Peter, James, and John, "He was transfigured. His face shone like the sun and His clothes became as white as light" (Matthew 17:1–2).

This brightness is not common to all glorified bodies in the same degree. All the bodies after the resurrection will be impassible, but their splendor will differ for each person. As explained by St. Paul, "The sun has its brightness, and the moon a different brightness, and the stars a different brightness, and the stars differ from each other in brightness. It is the same with the resurrection from the dead" (I Corinthians 15:41–42).

Agility is that quality of the risen body that frees it from the material burden that now presses it down. It will be able to move about with the greatest of ease and with a swiftness that depends only on the will. This is what the apostle meant when he said that our bodies are now sown in weakness, but on the last day they will be raised in power.

Subtility corresponds to what St. Paul calls "a spiritual body." Without ceasing to be material, that is extended in space and perceptible to the senses. The glorified body will be completely under the control of the spirit. It will be fully obedient to the soul.

If we look more closely at the foundation for these marvelous qualities of the risen body, we find them resulting from the soul's face-to-face vision of God. The beatific vision means just that. It beatifies; that is, makes the human soul perfectly happy in seeing the Holy Trinity. But it also beatifies the body with the soul in the indescribable joy of directly beholding the three Persons of the infinite Deity.

One closing observation on the state of the glorified body may answer some questions that come to mind. How will our bodies after the last day compare with the bodies we had on earth? The most detailed answer in Christian tradition is given in three whole chapters of St. Augustine's *City of God*. Only a few passages will be quoted here.

It is understood that no part of the body shall so perish as to produce deformity of the body. . . .

For all bodily beauty consists in the proportion of the parts; together, with a certain agreeableness of color. Where there is no proportion the eye is offended, either because there is something wanting, or too small, or too large. Consequently, there shall be no deformity resulting from want of proportion in that state in which all that is wrong is corrected, and all that is defective supplied from the resources which the Creator provides. All that is excessive will be removed without destroying the integrity of the substance. . . .

In the resurrection of the flesh, the body shall be of that size which it either had attained or should have attained in the flower of its youth, and shall enjoy the beauty that arises from symmetry and proportion in all its members (*The City of God,* III, 19–21).

There is great value in these reflections on the resurrection of the body. They help to sustain us as we go through life, by assuring us that our efforts are not in vain. Above all, they offer the promise of being glorified like Christ, provided we have endured like Him. In this we are encouraged by the first Bishop of Rome: "If you can have some share in the sufferings of Christ," he says, "be glad, because you will enjoy a much greater gladness when His glory is revealed" (I Peter 4:13). The secret is to believe this and to act on what we believe.

XII.

"LIFE EVERLASTING"

The closing article of the Apostles' Creed is also the opening door to our spiritual life. In fact, in one sense everlasting life is the spiritual life.

As understood in the Sacred Scriptures, eternal life begins at baptism (Romans 6:4). It is a new life, initiated by union with the death of Christ, which is symbolized and effected by baptism (Romans 6:4). It is death according to the flesh (Romans 8:12), but it is a resurrection from the life of sin (Romans 6:13). It is therefore a life conferred by holiness (Romans 5:18, 21). It is a life that is active within the Christian (I Corinthians 4:11). It is the conferral of the life of the Risen Jesus (Romans 8:11). We are thus reconciled with God by the death of Jesus, and saved by Him through a participation in His life (Romans 8:11). All of this is "everlasting life," while still in this world and before we enter into eternity.

There is more than passing value in seeing the two dimensions of everlasting life—here on earth and in the world to come. Not the least implication is that everlasting life is essentially the supernatural life.

Everlasting life is natural to God alone and belongs by right only to Him. It is beyond the natural, hence above (*super*) the rights or claims of any creature, whether angelic or human. It is nothing less than a participation in the very life of God, by grace here below and in glory in the heavens above.

The adjective "eternal" applied to life, therefore, means not only its endless duration after bodily death. It also signifies a share in God's own life, which is eternal because it is His life, uniquely His own.

Time and again the Scriptures not only speak of God as eternal, but identify Him as God because He alone in the absolute sense is eternal. Thus Abraham is said to have "invoked Yahweh, the Everlasting God" (Genesis 21:33). "He created the heavens and the earth. Although they wear out, He remains what He is and His years are never finished" (Psalm 102:26–28). The adjective "eternal" (Greek = *Aionios*) is applied to God to signify the kind of existence that transcends time (Romans 16:26).

God is the Alpha and the Omega—the first and the last letters of the Greek alphabet—because He is from everlasting unto everlasting (Revelation 1:8). He alone is without beginning because He always existed, and without end, because He will always exist. His very essence is to exist. He alone cannot not exist. And it is a share in this very life of the Trinity that we are privileged to possess in what we call time, and destined to enjoy, with God, when He calls us into eternal (*aionios*) life (Matthew 25:46).

Our focus here is on eternal life in "the life to

come," which is the closing article of the Nicene Creed. It is also the Church's main focus in her second millennium of commentary on the Apostles' Creed.

Heaven as the Vision of God

The Catholic Church identified heaven as the place and condition of perfect happiness. This happiness consists primarily in the immediate vision of God.

What is this immediate vision of God? In the Church's infallible teaching (Pope Benedict XII *Benedictus Deus,* 1336) the souls in heaven "see the divine essence with an intuitive and even face-to-face vision, without interposition of any creature" between God and the human soul. "Rather, the divine essence immediately manifests itself to them plainly, clearly, openly." As a result, "Those who see the divine essence in this way receive great joy from it." And because of this vision and enjoyment, the souls "are truly blessed and possess life and eternal rest."

Several words in this definition should be further explained:

1. The beatific vision of God is intuitive. This means that it is not the result of mental reasoning or reflection.

2. It is a face-to-face vision of the Blessed Trinity. Nothing stands between the soul and God.

3. It is direct perception of who God is, with no

creature as the channel or medium between the soul and its Creator.

4. It is so intimate that we may compare it with our knowledge of ourselves.

5. God reveals Himself plainly, openly, and clearly because He discloses Himself personally and not merely through the finite creatures He has made.

On earth, even our deepest knowledge of God is by contrast with the world that He made. But in heaven all this will be changed. "My dear people," the Apostle John wrote to the early Christians, "we are already the children of God. But what we are to be in the future has not yet been revealed. All we know is that when it is revealed we shall be like Him because we shall see Him as He really is" (I John 3:2). We shall behold the very reality of God.

Heavenly Enjoyment of God and of Creatures

Besides the immediate vision of God in heaven, we shall also enjoy creatures. This should not seem strange since, even on earth, God wants us to enjoy creatures—always, of course, subordinate to Himself.

At the summit of these created heavenly joys is the company and mutual love of the glorified Christ, the Blessed Virgin, the angels, and saints. Christ compared heaven to a wedding feast; He promised paradise to the good thief on Calvary; and He spoke of the many mansions that He went to heaven to prepare for us.

In heaven, we shall have the full use of our minds and wills. And after the resurrection our bodies will share in the heavenly joys. We may believe that knowledge we have acquired on earth will be carried into glory, along with the memory of past experiences, provided always that such knowledge will contribute to our happiness.

There is also communication of minds and the exchange of affections in heaven. Why? Because heaven is a society. As described by St. John, it is "the holy city and the new Jerusalem" (Revelation 21:2).

Few writers have improved on St. Thomas Aquinas's description of the joys of heaven in his *Exposition of the Apostles' Creed:*

> Eternal life is the perfect fulfillment of desire, because each of the blessed will have more than he desired or hoped for. In this life, no one can fulfill his desires, nor can any creature satisfy a man's craving. God alone satisfies and infinitely surpasses man's desires, which therefore can never rest except in God. "You have made us, O Lord, for yourself, and our heart is restless until it rests in you." (*Confessions,* 1) Since in heaven the saints possess God, it is evident that their desires are satisfied and their glory exceeds their expectations.
>
> [In commenting on our Lord's invitation to those on His right hand on the last day] "Enter

into the joy of the Lord," St. Augustine explains, that "their whole joy will not enter into the joyful, but the joyful will enter into joy."

"I shall be satisfied when your glory shall appear," sings the Psalmist, "who fills your desire with good things" (Psalm 16:15; 102:5). Why satisfied? Because whatsoever is delightful will be there superabundantly.

Our desire for pleasure will be perfectly fulfilled because we shall possess God, who is our sovereign Good.

Our desire for honor will be supremely achieved because all possible honor will be there.

Our desire for knowledge will be complete because in heaven we shall know the natures of all things. We shall know all truth and whatsoever we wish to know, we shall know. We shall possess whatever we wish to possess, together with eternal life.

Our desire for security will also be achieved, unlike the situation in this world. Here on earth there is no assured security. The more one has, and the higher one's position, the more reason there is to fear, and the more a person wants. But in life eternal, there is neither sorrow, nor toil, nor fear.

Our desire for pleasant companionship will be experienced in the company of all the blessed. Each person in heaven will share with others whatever he has, and all will love one another and rejoice in the happiness of everyone else. Thus the joy and gladness of each one will be as great as the joy of all.

St. Thomas makes sure we have no illusion about

the meaning of the alternative to eternal life as everlasting joy. In common with all the great commentators on the Apostles' Creed, he closes his exposition with a summary of the Church's teaching on hell.

The saints in heaven will have all these things and many more that surpass description. The wicked, on the other hand, will be in everlasting death. They will have no less sorrow and pain than the good will have joy and glory. Their punishment is aggravated in several ways:

—Through their separation from God and from all good things. This is the pain of loss, which corresponds to aversion, and surpasses the pain of sense.

—By the remorse of conscience. Yet their regret and anguish will be useless, for it will not be because of the hatred of sin, but because of the grief of their punishment.

—By the intensity of the pain of sense which is inflicted by the fires of hell and which will torture both soul and body. They will feel as though they are always dying, but never dead and never going to die. That is why it is described as everlasting death.

—By their despair of salvation. If only they could hope for deliverance from their agony, their punishment would be alleviated. But since they have lost all hope, their pains are exceedingly aggravated.

For nineteen hundred years, the Church's masters of the spiritual life have not ceased to dwell on this stark contrast between "everlasting life" and "everlasting death." Augustine and Francis of Assisi, Catherine of Siena and Teresa of Avila, Ignatius Loyola and Alphonsus Liguori, Thomas More and Maximilian Kolbe—all in their own way drew the obvious conclusion. There is an eternal difference between heaven and hell. "For this reason," says Aquinas, "man should often call these things to mind, since he is thereby urged to do good things and draw away from evil." That is why the Apostles' Creed ends with the words, "everlasting life," to make sure it becomes deeply impressed upon our memories.

"May we be brought to this life by our Lord Jesus Christ, who is God blessed for ever and ever. Amen." This is not only a prayer. It is the confident hope of everyone who professes the Apostles' Creed and puts it into practice.

PART TWO

CHANNELS
OF
GRACE

THE SACRAMENTS

The closing article of the Apostles' Creed, "I believe in life everlasting," is also the opening door to the seven sacraments instituted by Jesus Christ.

As we have seen, the eternal life that awaits those who believe in Christ is the supernatural life which He came into the world to restore to a fallen human race. That is why the Savior was so blunt in His explanation to Nicodemus about the need for being "born again".

> I tell you most solemnly, unless a man is born through water and the Spirit he cannot enter the kingdom of God. What is born of the flesh is flesh. What is born of the Spirit is spirit. Do not be surprised when I say: You must be born from above (John 3:5–7).

There are, therefore, two forms of birth because there are two levels of life. We acquire the natural life because we are born "out of human stock," and the "urge of the flesh, and the will of man." But there is a higher life whereby a person is born "of God Himself" (John 1:12–13).

The sacraments of the Catholic Church have all their meaning contained in this mystery of faith. The same Christ who said, "I have come that they may have life and have it to the full" (John 10:10), is the one who provided the principal means for obtaining, regaining and growing in this life—by instituting the sacraments of the New Law.

Channels of Divine Grace

Before we look into each of the sacraments, we should see more deeply what the Church understands by the supernatural life. In a word, by the supernatural life the Catholic Church understands the life of grace. And grace is the supernatural gift that God, of His free benevolence, bestows on human beings for their eternal salvation. The gifts of grace are essentially supernatural. They surpass the being, powers, and claims of created nature.

The variety of these gifts is beyond number, but they are ordinarily classified as sanctifying grace, the infused virtues, the gifts of the Holy Spirit, permanent character, and actual graces. All of these gifts are somehow received, restored, or increased by the sacraments of Jesus Christ.

Sanctifying Grace. The most fruitful term in revelation for sanctifying grace is simply "life." In the original Greek of the New Testament, it is regularly called *zoe*, in preference to two other words for "life" in Greek, namely, *bios* and *psyche*. The New Testament understands *zoe* to mean the supernatural life that God communicates to us through Christ.

Most often, the combination *zoe aionios*, eternal life, is found in the gospels and St. Paul. Yet the same *zoe* that we possess on earth as divine grace will continue in eternity as heavenly glory. This is the divine life that was in the Word from the beginning and "from His fullness we have, all of us, received—yes, grace in return for grace" (John 1:16).

In technical language, we may say that the divine indwelling in the souls of the just is the Uncreated Grace of the Holy Trinity. The created effect of this indwelling is sanctifying grace.

St. Augustine speaks of sanctifying grace as the "soul of the soul." He means that our body has the soul as its source (or principle) of natural life. So our soul has its source of supernatural life, which is sanctifying grace.

Thus sanctifying grace is a divine quality inhering in the soul. From this follows a number of wonderful effects.

1. Sanctifying grace makes the soul holy and pleasing to God. St. Paul wrote to the early Christians: "You are washed; you are sanctified; you are justified, in the name of our Lord Jesus Christ and the Spirit of our God" (I Corinthians 6:11). Sanctity means freedom from mortal sin, and pos-

itively it is the enduring supernatural union with God.

2. Sanctifying grace makes the soul supernaturally beautiful. As a sharing in the very nature of God, it produces in the soul an image of the Uncreated Beauty of the Holy Trinity. It remolds the soul to the likeness of Christ, who is "the radiant light of God's glory" (Hebrews 1:3).

3. Sanctifying grace makes us friends of God. On entering the soul, it changes one from an unjust person into a just person, and from an enemy into a friend of God. As Jesus told the apostles: "You are my friends if you do what I command you. I shall not call you servants any more because a servant does not know his master's business. I call you friends because I have made known to you everything I have learned from my Father" (John 15:14–15).

4. Sanctifying grace makes us *children* of God and *heirs* of heaven. The two privileges go together. "Everyone," says St. Paul, "moved by the Spirit is a son of God. The spirit you received is not the spirit of slaves bringing fear into your lives. It is the spirit of sons and it makes us cry out, 'Abba, Father!' The Spirit Himself and our spirit united witness that we are children of God. And if we are children, we are heirs as well: heirs of God and co-heirs with Christ, sharing His sufferings so as to share His glory" (Romans 8:14–17). That is why a person who dies in sanctifying grace may be said to have a right to heaven. It is

the right of inheritance given to us through the merits of Christ's Passion.

5. Sanctifying grace makes a person a temple of the Holy Spirit. How so? The reason is that the Holy Spirit dwells in the souls of the just not only by means of His created gifts of grace that He confers. Rather, He abides in the soul by His un-created Divine Nature. "Do you not know," St. Paul asks, "that you are the temple of God and that the Spirit of God dwells in you . . . Holy is the temple of God, and this temple you are" (I Corinthians 3:16–17).

Infused Virtue. It is the infallible teaching of the Church that the virtues of faith, hope, and charity are conferred along with sanctifying grace.

These virtues are received in the soul as perma-nent habits or dispositions. The Church says they are infused. This is to make clear that they are not ac-quired, as are other habits, by repetition of an act. They must be, as it were, directly "poured in" (in-fundere) by God.

The virtue of faith enables us to assent with our minds to everything which God has revealed. Our motive for accepting God's revelation is His own di-vine authority. We believe because He is all-knowing and therefore cannot be deceived, and all good, and therefore would not deceive us. When He tells us something we accept His word as infallibly true.

The virtue of hope belongs to the will. It makes a person desire eternal life, which is the heavenly vision of God, and gives one the confidence of receiving the grace necessary to reach heaven. The grounds of hope are God's almighty power, His infinite goodness, and His fidelity to what He promised.

The virtue of charity enables us to love God for His own sake and to love others out of love for God. Like hope, charity resides in the human will. But unlike hope, charity is selfless love. When we hope, we also love God, but we love Him because of the reward we justly expect of Him—grace in this life and eternal glory in the life to come.

But charity is different than hope. The English word "love" does not fully express what we mean by charity. Love may be natural or supernatural. Charity is uniquely supernatural. Love is often equated with "like," which implies a natural attraction. Charity may be practiced even in the absence of such spontaneous appeal. Love commonly involves our internal emotions and usually implies a depth of feeling. Charity does not exclude emotions or feelings, but, in essence charity, is a virtue of the free will. It goes out to the object which we love, either God or our neighbor, in order to please the one who is loved.

The virtues of faith, hope, and charity are called theological because their immediate object is God (*Theos* in Greek). They are directed to Him. We believe in Him who is the Truth, we hope in Him who is the Way, and we love Him who is the Life.

But there are four other virtues that are called moral because their immediate object is human behavior (from the Latin *mores*, meaning fixed, morally binding customs). They are also called cardinal virtues (from the Latin *cardo*, hinge) because they are like hinges on which all the moral virtues depend.

There are four basic moral virtues, namely prudence in the intellect, and justice, fortitude, and temperance in the will. It is the Church's common teaching that, along with the theological virtues the moral virtues are also infused into the soul with sanctifying grace.

Gifts of the Holy Spirit. Along with the infused virtues, a person who receives sanctifying grace also receives the seven gifts of the Holy Spirit. They are seven forms of supernatural instincts or initiatives which prompt a person to respond to the divine movements of grace.

The gifts are like reflexes that enable a person to spontaneously answer to the impulses of God's grace. Their scriptural basis is the prophetic endowment of the Messiah.

> The spirit of the Lord shall rest upon Him, the spirit of wisdom, and of understanding, the spirit of counsel and of fortitude, the spirit of knowledge and of godliness. And He shall be filled with the spirit of the fear of the Lord (Isaiah 11:2–3).

Although directly attributed to the Messiah these gifts are implicitly the common possession of all Christians, whose very name signifies "Messianists" (*Mashiah*, Hebrew for Anointed, which in Greek is *Christos*).

Four of the gifts of the Holy Spirit belong to the intellect—wisdom, understanding, knowledge, and counsel; and three to the will—fortitude, piety, and fear of the Lord. They are different from the virtues in that they prompt the virtues into action and, when faithfully responded to, enable a person to perform extraordinary, even heroic, deeds after the example of Jesus Christ.

Permanent Character. Three of the sacraments confer an indelible character on the soul. Thus Baptism, Confirmation and Holy Orders imprint a permanent, supernatural quality on the person, which differs for each of these sacraments. But they have one effect in common: They assimilate a person to the priesthood of Christ in a special way.

The sacramental character is indelible. This means that it remains in a person who may have lost sanctifying grace or even the virtue of faith.

The sacramental character is called a character because it permanently seals the person with a supernatural quality, similar (though on a higher level) to the character that identifies each individual as a distinct personality. Moreover, it is called a character because it permanently gives the one who receives it certain powers that no one else possesses.

In philosophical terms, the sacramental character changes the one who receives it in his very being. Persons baptized, confirmed, or ordained are forever new beings. They have a unique relationship to Christ that no one else has, and they are empowered to do things that no one else can perform.

Logically, too, the sacramental character is conferred only once. Consequently the sacraments which bestow the character can never be repeated. A person remains baptized, confirmed, and ordained into eternity.

Actual Graces. The best way to understand the meaning of actual graces is to compare them with God's constant influence on our created nature. Just as we could not use our natural powers without continued divine support, so we need the help of His grace to retain or grow in the supernatural life of God.

Actual graces therefore are temporary influences from God that enlighten our minds and inspire our wills to perform supernatural actions that lead to heaven.

One of the great blessings of the sacraments is that they are the richest source of actual graces available to mankind. It is mainly through the sacraments that God provides His people with the holy thoughts and holy desires they need to enable them to reach heaven.

Each sacrament has its own treasury of actual graces available to those who receive the sacraments. Moreover, as we shall see, the Holy Eucharist as a Sacrifice and a Presence sacrament mysteriously supplies graces even to those who are not Christian believers or may be sinners totally estranged from God.

What Are the Sacraments?

We may define a sacrament as a visible sign instituted by Christ which effectively communicates the grace it signifies.

Each of the seven sacraments is something visible or sensibly perceptible. The water poured in Baptism, the oil used in Confirmation, the bread and wine for the Eucharist, along with the words pronounced and the ritual seen, are all perceptible to the senses.

The sacraments are not only perceived by the senses: They are also signs which signify. They manifest something beyond the visible ritual performed. Thus water signifies washing, oil signifies strengthening or healing, eating and drinking signify being nourished. In each case the external sign signifies some internal change taking place in the human spirit. And always this change is in the supernatural order, including some area or aspect of divine grace.

But the sacraments are not merely signs that grace is received. No, the heart of the sacraments is that they actually produce the grace which they signify. They are like instruments in the hands of Christ who, through them, confers the graces proper to each sacrament.

Over the centuries the Catholic Church has had to defend the fact that Christ Himself instituted all seven sacraments. He did so personally and immediately. He determined the substance of each sacrament; its essential ritual and content; who is empowered to confer the sacraments, and on whom they may be conferred; what material is to be used; and essentially how each sacrament is to be an effective sign of grace.

As Catholics, we recognize two sources of divine revelation, Sacred Scripture and Sacred Tradition. Consequently we do not expect to find explicit evidence in the Bible for Christ's institution of all the sacraments. No matter. The Church teaches infallibly that "the sacraments of the New Law were all instituted by Christ," that "these same sacraments of the New Law differ from the sacraments of the Old Law," and that "there are neither more than seven nor fewer than seven sacraments" (Council of Trent, March 3, 1547).

How necessary are the sacraments? They are necessary for salvation, even if not all are necessary for each individual. The actual reception of a sacrament can, in case of necessity, be replaced by at least the implicit desire for the sacrament.

The Second Vatican Council declared that Christ established the Church "as the universal sacrament of salvation" (*Constitution on the Church*, VII). Among other things, this means that the sacraments of the Church are somehow necessary for the salvation of the world.

Absolutely speaking, God, who is almighty and perfectly free, could have chosen to confer grace without the sacraments. Why then, did He choose to dispense His grace through the sacraments? He did so in order that the mysterious effects of His infinite power should be made intelligible by means of cer-

125

tain signs that are evident to our senses. If we were disembodied spirits, God might have dispensed His graces directly, without the use of material things. But since we are creatures of body and soul, God chose to use bodily means to confer His spiritual blessings on our souls. Christ instituted the sacraments because He knew how much we depend on external, visible signs to sustain our faith in His promises.

Moreover, the sacraments are a continuation of Christ's work of redemption. They are the link, as it were, between His Passion on Calvary and our present needs on earth. They are the channels by which His saving merits are now conveyed to a sinful world.

The sacraments provide a marvelous bond of visible unity among the members of Christ's Church. They distinguish the followers of Christ from all others, while those who belong to the Mystical Body are thus joined together by a sacred bond.

By means of the sacraments we make a public profession of our faith, and others witness to what we profess to believe. In this way our faith is strengthened by its external profession and our charity is deepened by sharing with others, and they with us, the sacred mysteries of Christianity.

Finally the sacraments afford us a constant check on our pride. They encourage us to the practice of humility by making us submit to material things as a condition for obtaining the graces that we need for the spiritual life.

BAPTISM

Baptism was already prefigured in the Old Testament. Some of the ancient rites or events that anticipated Christian Baptism were circumcision (Colossians 2:11), the march of the Israelites through the Red Sea (I Corinthians 10:2), and across the Jordan (Joshua 3:14). What the Church considers a formal prophecy of baptism was the oracle of Ezekiel regarding the New Israel.

> I shall pour clean water over you and you will be cleansed. I shall cleanse you of all defilement and all your idols. I shall give you a new heart and put a new spirit in you (Ezekiel 36:25).

An immediate preparation for the Baptism instituted by Christ was the baptism administered by St. John, which moved those who received it to repentance for their sins. This in turn prepared them for divine forgiveness. But John's baptism did not itself remove sins, unlike the sacrament of Baptism which directly causes the remission of the guilt and punishment of all sin.

Institution by Christ

We cannot tell from the Scriptures exactly when Christ instituted the first sacrament. According to St. Bonaventure, the Savior decided on the material to be used when He was Himself baptized by John in the Jordan; He began to communicate the graces of baptism when He rose from the dead; He determined how the sacrament should be given when He commanded the apostles to baptize in the name of the Holy Trinity; He merited the graces to be conferred at baptism during His Passion and death on the Cross; and He foretold its purpose and necessity, during His conversation with Nicodemus as recorded in the Fourth Gospel (John 3:1–21).

A Catholic may not doubt that Christ instituted the sacrament of Baptism or say "that the Roman Church, which is the mother and teacher of all churches, does not have the true doctrine concerning the sacrament of Baptism" (Council of Trent, March 3, 1547).

The Church's teaching on this sacrament is precise and extensive. One reason is that Baptism is the most fundamental of the seven sacraments. We may say it is also a model for all the sacraments in terms of their power to confer or deepen the supernatural life of the soul.

To understand how Baptism operates is to see

how all the sacraments are effective signs of divine grace.

What Is Baptism?

A very clear and up-to-date definition of this sacrament is provided by the new Code of Canon Law issued by Pope John Paul II on January 25, 1983, the feast of the conversion of St. Paul. After quoting the definition, we shall briefly analyze its principal elements.

> Baptism, the gateway to the sacraments, is necessary for salvation by actual reception or at least by desire. By it people are freed from sins, are born again as children of God and, made like to Christ by an indelible character, are incorporated into the Church. It is validly conferred only by a washing in real water with the proper form of words used (Canon 849).

The first thing that strikes us in this definition is that Baptism is the gateway (Latin *janua* = door) to the sacraments. In other words, no other sacraments can be received except by a person who has been baptized.

It means that a baptized person has a unique title which belongs to no one else. It is the title to those graces which Christ reserves exclusively to baptized people. Even if a person has lost God's friendship through grave sin, and perhaps lost every vestige of faith by denying God's revealed truth, yet the ability to receive the other sacraments remains. This, of course, presumes that the necessary conditions are fulfilled.

In saying that baptism is necessary for salvation, the Church is telling us that the obligation applies to all human beings without exception. Unless they are reborn through the grace of baptism, they cannot attain the beatific vision.

Christ's teaching on the universal necessity of baptism has been interpreted by the Church to mean that in case of emergency baptism by water can be replaced by baptism of desire or baptism by blood. Baptism of desire is the explicit or at least implicit desire for sacramental baptism and is associated with perfect sorrow for one's sins, that is, contrition based on charity or the love of God. Baptism of blood means the patient endurance of a violent death because of one's profession of the Christian faith or the practice of Christian virtue. Even young childern can receive baptism of blood, as is clear from the Church's honoring the Holy Innocents who entered heaven after they were murdered by Herod at the time of Christ's birth in Bethlehem.

The Church has never wavered, however, in insisting that even children before the age of reason must receive baptism of water. Thus, in the famous definition of Pope Benedict XII referred to before, he states explicitly which persons attain to the beatific vision. They are the souls of "all the saints" who died before the Passion of Christ. They are also those of the "faithful who died after receiving the

Holy Baptism of Christ," provided they needed no
purification after death or had been duly purified in
purgatory. Then the crucial statement that, "The
same is true of the souls of children who have been
reborn in Baptism when they die before attaining the
use of free will" (Constitution *Blessed God,* January
29, 1336).

This historic declaration is introduced by the
words, "According to the usual providence of God."
Consequently, we leave to God's mercy the eternal
destiny of those who die without baptism before
reaching the age of discretion. But historically the
Church has never given her official approval to any
theory that substitutes for infants some other way of
attaining the beatific vision other than baptism of
water. Moreover, the Church has condemned as
"false", the Jansenist denial of a limbo of children.
This would be a place of perfect, natural happiness
but without the face-to-face vision of God (Pope Pius
VI, in *The Author of Faith,* August 28, 1794).

The Church's law on the duty of baptizing infants is emphatic.

> Parents are obliged to see that their infants
> are baptized within the first few weeks. As soon as
> possible after the birth, indeed, even before it
> they are to approach the parish priest to ask for
> the sacrament for their child.

In fact "if the infant is in danger of death, it is to
be baptized without delay" (Canon 867).

Effects of Baptism

The Church identifies four main effects of the sacrament of Baptism, namely: removal of sin, rebirth as a child of God, assimilation to Christ, and incorporation into the Church. Each of these deserves at least a short explanation.

Removal of Sin. The best way to explain the removal of sin by Baptism is to understand that the sacrament confers divine grace.

After all, this is what really happened when our first parents sinned. They lost the supernatural life and virtues and gifts they had possessed before they fell. By their sin they lost these graces not only for themselves but for their descendants.

What then, does Baptism do? It restores the essential graces that Adam and Eve did not pass on to their posterity. By restoring these graces Baptism removes the inherited sin.

What graces are restored? All the supernatural gifts which our first parents had in what we call "original justice." Baptism restores the uncreated grace of the Indwelling Trinity, sanctifying grace, the infused theological virtues, and the gifts of the Holy Spirit.

Restored too, are the fruits (Latin *frui*, to enjoy) of the Holy Spirit which are the enjoyable experiences we have when we put the virtues and gifts into action. St. Paul identifies twelve such experiences when he compares "the works of the flesh" with their

132

opposites. "The fruit of the Spirit" he says, "is charity, joy, peace, patience, benignity, goodness, longanimity, mildness, faith, modesty, continency, chastity" (Galatians 5:22–23). This is not an exhaustive list of the fruits of the Holy Spirit. It is rather a series of examples of virtues that when practiced, give us spiritual ease and satisfaction in doing the will of God.

If the person baptized is older and therefore has committed personal sins, these too are totally removed, both in their guilt (or loss of grace) and their penalty (suffering due). This includes the remission of all mortal sins along with their debt of eternal punishment.

Supernatural Rebirth. In positive terms, the sacrament of Baptism makes us adopted children of a loving God.

There is only one natural conception and birth for us human beings. But thanks to the suffering and death of Jesus Christ we have access to a second origin as adopted children of God's own divine community, which is the Holy Trinity. This second now supernatural origin takes place the moment we are baptized.

Likeness to Christ. What makes us like Christ is the indelible character we described in our earlier reflections on the sacraments in general. As we saw, the sacraments of Baptism, Confirmation and Holy Orders each confer their own distinctive supernatural character.

The distinctive quality of the baptismal character is to give a person a twofold share in Christ's own priestly power. The first is a share in Christ's power to offer Himself in sacrifice to the heavenly Father. The second is a share in Christ's power to communicate to others the graces that He gained for the world by His death on Calvary.

Incorporation into the Church. The two expressions "incorporation into Christ" and "incorporation into the Church" are used almost interchangeably. Yet there is some difference between them.

Incorporation by Baptism into Christ is basically what we mean by being assimilated to Christ's priesthood, as just described.

Incorporation into the Church builds on being incorporated into Christ. But it goes beyond this. Baptism makes a person part of the Mystical Body of Christ which is His Church. The one baptized receives certain rights and privileges, and duties that no one else can claim. Christ who is the Head of His Church works on those who are baptized and through them to continue His great work of salvation. In a profound sense, they are a continued extension, or an extended continuation, of Himself as Redeemer of the human race.

Whatever a baptized person does for the rest of his life on earth builds on this foundation. Why? Because Baptism entitles a person to a lifetime of extraordinary actual graces that no one else can expect to receive from God.

The Ritual of Baptism

The essential rite of Baptism has not changed since Christ told His disciples: "All power is given to me in heaven and on earth. Go, therefore, teach all nations, baptizing them in the name of the Father, and of the Son, and of the Holy Spirit" (Matthew 28:18–19).

No significant liturgical change was introduced by the Second Vatican Council. However, certain modifications were made to the new Code of Canon Law. Only two ways of baptizing are now allowed, namely "by immersion or by pouring." Previously Canon Law offered a third option, by sprinkling (Canon 854).

Also, previously it was required that a Christian name be given to the one being baptized. The new Code simply says that "a name foreign to a Christian mentality is not given" (Canon 855).

CONFIRMATION

"If there was ever a time when the Sacrament of Confirmation needed to be explained carefully, that time is now. All too many members of the Church neglect it altogether; and those who have received it or who plan to receive it, see it as something minor in their lives. There is need, then, for instruction on the nature, power, and dignity of this sacrament. Far from being neglected or received in a mere perfunctory way, Confirmation must be restored to the reverence and devotion it deserves."

These words introduced *The Roman Catechism* published by Pope St. Pius V in 1566. They might just as appropriately have been written today.

Institution by Christ

There is no direct evidence in Scripture that Christ actually instituted the sacrament of Confirmation. Yet the Church has formally defined that Christ personally instituted this sacrament. Indeed the Council of Trent went out of its way to teach as irreversible Catholic doctrine that "the Confirmation of baptized persons is . . . a true and proper sacrament." It simply rejected the notion that confirmation "meant nothing more than a certain catechesis by which those nearing adolescence gave an account of their faith before the Church" (*Decree on the Sacraments,* March 3, 1547).

Already in the Old Covenant the prophets foretold that outpouring of the Spirit of God over the whole of humanity as one of the distinctive signs of the messianic age.

Jesus plainly promised to send the Holy Spirit, and went on to describe the effect this would have on His followers.

> I shall ask the Father and He will give you another Advocate to be with you forever, that Spirit of truth whom the world can never receive since it neither sees nor knows Him (John 14:16–17).
>
> I have said these things to you while still with you. But the Advocate, the Holy Spirit, whom the Father will send in my name, will teach you everything, and bring all things to your mind that I have said to you (John 14:25–26).

On the way to His ascension, Christ finally promised to send the Holy Spirit soon. He told the disciples not to leave Jerusalem but to "wait there for what the Father had promised." He reminded them:

"It is what you have heard me speak about. John baptized with water but you, not many days from now, will be baptized with the Holy Spirit." Then still more clearly, He predicted what the Holy Spirit would do in their lives. "You will receive power," Christ assured them, "when the Holy Spirit comes on you, and then you will be my witnesses not only in Jerusalem but throughout Judea and Samaria and indeed to the ends of the earth" (Acts 1:4–5, 8). Note that the Greek word for "witnesses" in the inspired text of the Acts of the Apostles is *martures* which means "martyrs." The kind of witnessing that Christ's followers will be empowered by the Holy Spirit to give is to martyrdom.

What the apostles themselves received on Pentecost Sunday, they soon began to communicate to others. The rite they used was the imposition of hands on the newly baptized.

> When the apostles in Jerusalem heard that Samaria had accepted the word of God, they sent Peter and John to them. And they went down there, and prayed for the Samaritans to receive the Holy Spirit, for as yet He had not come down on any of them. They had only been baptized in the name of the Lord Jesus. Then they laid hands on them, and they received the Holy Spirit (Acts 8:14–17).

Later on in the Acts of the Apostles, we are told that St. Paul imposed his hands on some twelve converts who had been baptized and they received the Holy Spirit (Acts 19:6).

So the practice continued through the apostolic age into the early Christian centuries. And always the understanding was that Confirmation was a sacrament distinct from Baptism; that it consisted in the imposition of hands by the apostles and their successors; that the effect of the outward rite was a special communication of the Holy Spirit, the divine source of interior sanctification.

What Is Confirmation?

As we did for the sacrament of Baptism, we will examine the meaning of Confirmation in the words of the new Code of Canon Law. It contains all the essential elements of this second of the seven sacraments.

> The sacrament of Confirmation confers a character. By it the baptized continue their path of Christian initiation. They are enriched with the gift of the Holy Spirit, and are more closely linked to the Church. They are made strong and more firmly obliged by word and deed to witness to Christ and to spread and defend the faith.

Immediately we see that Confirmation is exactly what its name implies. It is the sacrament which makes *firm* or strengthens the gifts of grace that are first received in Baptism.

Sacramental Character. The Church stresses that the indelible seal received in Confirmation is really a new character. It is not merely a deepening of the baptismal character. The Church's tradition teaches that the confirmation character gives the power and the right to perform actions which are necessary in the spiritual battle against the enemies of the faith. These enemies are the world, our own proud intellect and will, and the evil spirit.

Moreover, the Church does not hesitate to say that Confirmation changes the simple members of the kingdom of Christ into soldiers of Christ. St. Ignatius, in his *Spiritual Exercises,* expresses this idea forcefully in the invitation that Christ extends to His chosen followers.

> My will is to conquer the whole world and all enemies and thus to enter into the glory of my Father. Whoever, therefore, desires to come with me must labor with me in order that following me in pain, he may likewise follow me in glory (*The Kingdom of Christ*).

The character of Confirmation confers on the baptized the strength they need to live up to Christ's expectations of the Mystical Body on earth, which is the Church Militant.

Sacramental Graces. Consistent with the distinctive character of Confirmation, a variety of special graces is assured for a lifetime loyalty to Christ and His Church.

Along with Baptism, Confirmation is a sacrament of initiation. It lays the foundation, after Baptism, for living up to the hard demands of the gospel.

Confirmation binds the one baptized more intimately to the Church, which means more closely to Christ, and enables us to be more devoted to His divine Person and to serve Him more faithfully.

Three words in the Church's definition of Confirmation bring out the unique effects of this sacrament. They are to *"witness* to Christ," and *"spread* and *defend* the faith." On each of these three levels, Confirmation strengthens a Christian and imposes the obligation to witness, spread, and defend. Let us now examine them in detail.

1. In order to be able to witness to Christ, confirmation deepens a person's faith by making Christ better understood, more clearly perceived, and more firmly believed in as the Son of the living God who became man to redeem the world. In a word, Confirmation strengthens our conviction of mind by enabling us to say with St. Paul: "I have not lost confidence, because I know who it is that I have put my trust in, and I have no doubt at all that He is able to take care of all that I have entrusted to Him until that Day" (II Timothy 1:12).

Conviction is the bedrock of courage: A convinced mind is the foundation for a courageous will. Every courageous witness to Christ was, in effect, a martyr for Christ, either by shedding his blood for the Savior in dying a martyr's death, or certainly testifying to his deathless love for Christ by living a martyr's life.

2. In order to be able to spread the faith, Confirmation develops our sense of mission and deepens our desire to share with others what others have so zealously passed on to us.

St. John Chrysostom is warrant for the statement that, on the last day, we shall be judged mainly on our practice of charity in sharing our Catholic faith. The Second Vatican Council expressed the same idea in its *Decree on the Apostolate of Lay People.*

From the fact of their union with Christ the Head, flows the laymen's right and duty to be apostles. Inserted as they are in the Mystical Body by Baptism and strengthened by the power of the Holy Spirit in Confirmation, it is by the Lord Himself that they are assigned to the apostolate (I, 3).

The council goes so far as to say that a Catholic "who does not work at the growth of the Body [of Christ] to the extent of his possibilities must be considered useless both to the Church and himself" (I, 2). The apostolate is therefore no option but a grave obligation.

3. In order to be able to defend the faith, Confirmation does two things: It enlightens the mind

of the believer to know how the true faith should be protected from danger or against assault, and it fortifies the will to want to come to the defense of the faith at no matter what cost to one's self-love or ease.

This defense of Catholic truth should always, of course, be done with prudence and charity. That is why our zeal must be tempered by wisdom and love. But the basic obligation remains.

One final observation. The faithful are told that Confirmation deepens their duty "to witness to Christ and to spread and defend the faith." They are also told how to fulfill this triple responsibility: They are to do so "by word and deed."

These two, word and deed, go together. No less than Christ Himself, during His visible stay on earth, proclaimed the gospel by what He said and what He did, so those who have been confirmed by His Spirit are to follow His example. Both verbal communication and the practice of Christian virtue are the means of testifying to the Savior, of extending His kingdom on earth, and of safeguarding the treasures of revealed truth which God became man to share with the human family.

Ritual and Administration

Six years after the close of the Second Vatican Council, Pope Paul VI determined by his pontifical authority that the essence of Confirmation consists in both the imposition of hands and the anointing with chrism. He also determined that the words of confirmation should be almost identical with those used by the Catholic Church in the Eastern or Byzantine rite:

> By our supreme apostolic authority, we decree and lay down that in the Latin Church the following should be observed in the future: The sacrament of Confirmation is conferred through the anointing with chrism on the forehead, which is done by the laying on of the hand and through the words, "Receive the seal of the Gift of the Holy Spirit" (*Apostolic Constitution*, August 15, 1971).

The ordinary minister of Confirmation is the bishop. Priests can also administer Confirmation provided they have the faculty by the Church's common law or have been duly authorized to confirm. One of the new provisions of Canon Law gives priests the power to confirm those whom they have instructed in the faith and received into the Church. In danger of death the pastor and, in fact, any priest can confer the sacrament of Confirmation.

Absolutely speaking, "All baptized persons who have not been confirmed, and only they, are capable of receiving Confirmation." However, to be lawfully confirmed a person should have the use of reason, be suitably instructed, properly disposed, and able to renew the baptismal promises (Canon 889). The Church's general law is that "the sacrament of Confirmation is to be conferred at about the age of discretion." The conference of bishops may determine another age. The age for Confirmation may be further qualified by the judgment of the one who is to confer the sacrament or when there is danger of death (Canon 891).

We should add, however, that Confirmation can be received by any baptized person before reaching the age of reason. This is clear from the practice of confirming infants in the west up to the thirteenth century and today in the Eastern Church. Corresponding to its purpose of enabling a baptized person to be a *miles Christi*, "soldier of Christ," the Latin Rite has decided that Confirmation should be delayed until after infancy. However, as noted before, exceptions are admissible, especially in danger of death. It should always be kept in mind that Confirmation provides a person with a higher state of grace on earth and, as a result, a higher state of glory in eternity.

THE EUCHARIST

The Holy Eucharist is unique among the sacraments. Even the variety of names by which it is called emphasizes the central position which it occupies in Catholic Christianity. It is the Blessed Sacrament, the Lord's Supper, the Holy of Holies, the Table of the Lord, the Body and Blood of Christ, the Sacrifice of the Mass, Holy Communion, the Sacrament of the Altar, Viaticum, and the Real Presence—to mention only a few of the titles by which the Church has identified this central Mystery of Faith.

Yet among the names that have come down to us, the most favored is the "Eucharist," from the Greek word *Eucharistia*, which means "Thanksgiving." It appears already in the writings of St. Ignatius of Antioch (died 107 A.D.) and St. Justin, Martyr (died 165 A.D.).

We may say there are three cardinal mysteries of the Christian religion, namely, the Trinity, the Incarnation, and the Eucharist. Among these the Eucharist implies the other two, since without the Trinity there would have been no Incarnation, and without the Incarnation there would have been no Eucharist.

Our purpose here is mainly to consider the Eucharist as a sacrament that is a visible sign instituted by Christ, which effectively produces the grace it signifies. Yet in reflecting on the Eucharist as a sacrament, we must keep in mind what Pope John Paul II said in the first encyclical he wrote as Bishop of Rome.

> The Church lives by the Eucharist, by the fullness of this sacrament, the stupendous content and meaning of which have often been expressed in the Church's magisterium from the most distant times down to our own days. . . .
>
> Indeed, the Eucharist is the ineffable sacrament! The essential commitment and, above all, the visible grace and source of supernatural strength for the Church as the People of God is to persevere and advance constantly in Eucharistic life and Eucharistic piety, and to develop spiritually in the climate of the Eucharist. . . .
>
> With all the greater reason, then, it is not permissible for us, in thought, life, or action to take away from this truly most Holy Sacrament its full magnitude and its essential meaning. . . .
>
> It is at one and the same time a sacrifice-sacrament, a communion-sacrament, and a Presence-sacrament (*The Redeemer of Man*, IV, 20).

Consequently, although the Eucharist is one sacrament, it is a sacrament in three distinctive ways as sacrifice, communion, and Presence. We shall examine each of these in sequence, while seeing how each one relates to the other two.

Eucharist as Sacrifice-Sacrament

The most serious challenge to the Catholic faith in the Eucharist was the claim that the Mass is not a real but merely a symbolic sacrifice.

To defend this basic Eucharistic mystery, the Council of Trent made a series of definitions. Originally drafted as negative anathemas, they may be reduced to the following positive affirmation of faith.

1. The Mass is a true and proper sacrifice which is offered to God.

2. By the words, "Do this in commemoration of me" (Luke 22:19; I Corinthians 11:24), Christ made the apostles priests. Moreover, He decreed that they and other priests should offer His Body and Blood.

3. The Sacrifice of the Mass is not merely an offering of praise and thanksgiving, or simply a memorial of the sacrifice on the Cross. It is a propitiatory sacrifice which is offered for the living and dead, for the remission of sins and punishment due to sin, as satisfaction for sin and for other necessities.

4. The Sacrifice of the Mass in no way detracts from the sacrifice which Christ offered on the Cross (Council of Trent, Session XXII, September 17, 1562).

Volumes of teaching by the Church's magisterium have been written since the Council of Trent. There has also been a remarkable development of doctrine in a deeper understanding of the Mass. For our purpose, there are especially two questions that need to be briefly answered: 1) How is the Sacrifice of the Mass related to the sacrifice of the Cross? 2) How is the Mass a true sacrifice?

Relation of the Mass to Calvary. In order to see how the Mass is related to Calvary, we must immediately distinguish between the actual Redemption of the world and the communication of Christ's redemptive graces to a sinful human race.

On the Cross, Christ really redeemed the human family. He is the one true Mediator between God and an estranged humanity. On the Cross, He merited all the graces that the world would need to be reconciled with an offended God.

When He died, the separation of His blood from His body caused the separation of His human soul from the body, which caused His death. He willed to die in the deepest sense of the word. He chose to die. In His own words, He laid down His life for the salvation of a sinful mankind.

But His physical death on Calvary was not to be an automatic redemption of a sin-laden world. It would not exclude the need for us to appropriate the merits He gained on the Cross; nor would it exclude the need for our voluntary cooperation with the graces merited by the Savior's shedding of His blood.

The key to seeing the relation between Calvary

and the Mass is the fact that the same identical Jesus Christ now glorified is present on the altar at Mass as He was present in His mortal humanity on the Cross.

Since it is the same Jesus, we must say He continues in the Mass what He did on Calvary except that now in the Mass, He is no longer mortal or capable of suffering in His physical person. On Calvary He was, by His own choice, capable of suffering and dying. What He did then was to gain the blessings of our redemption. What He does now in the Mass is apply these blessings to the constant spiritual needs of a sinful, suffering humanity.

Before we look more closely at the Mass as a sacrifice of propitiation and petition, we should make plain that it is first and foremost, a sacrifice of praise (adoration) and thanksgiving. No less than He did on Calvary, in the Mass Jesus continues to offer Himself to the heavenly Father. Since the highest form of honor to God is sacrifice, the Mass is a continuation of Christ's sacrifice of praise and gratitude to God the Father. But, whereas on Calvary, this sacrificial adoration was bloody, causing Christ's physical death by crucifixion, in the Mass the same Jesus is now sacrificing Himself in an unbloody manner because He is now glorified, immortal, and incapable of suffering or dying in His own physical person.

We now turn from the Mass as a sacrifice of adoration and thanks (referring to God), to the Mass as a sacrifice of propitiation and petition (referring to us).

Notice we use two words, *propitiation* and *petition*. They are not the same.

1. The Mass is the most powerful means we have to obtain propitiation for sin. This occurs in different ways.

- Through the Mass, God's mercy makes reparation for the want of divine love that we have shown by committing sin.

- Through the Mass, God's mercy removes the guilt of repented venial sins and moves the sinner estranged from Him to return to God.

- Through the Mass, God's mercy remits more or less of the punishment still due on earth to forgiven sins.

- Through the Mass, God's mercy also remits more or less of the punishment which the souls in purgatory have to undergo before entering heaven.

2. The Mass is a powerful means of petition to God for the graces that we and others need in our pilgrimage through life.

- Graces are necessary for the mind to know what is God's will and how it should be fulfilled.

- Graces are necessary for the will to desire what pleases God, to choose what He wants us to do, and to sustain our choice by loving Him above all things.

In both ways, as a means of propitiation and petition, the Mass is a sacrament. It confers the graces needed from God's mercy to expiate the sins of the past, and the graces needed from God's bounty to obtain His blessings for the future.

The Mass a True Sacrifice. Since the first century of her existence, the Church has considered the Mass a sacrifice. The earliest manual of the liturgy (before 90 A.D.) has this directive for the attendance of Sunday Mass.

> On the Lord's own day, assemble in common to break bread and offer thanks. But first confess your sins so that your sacrifice may be pure. However, no one quarreling with his brother may join your meeting until they are reconciled; your sacrifice must not be defiled (*Teaching of the Twelve Apostles*, 14).

Why is the Mass a true sacrifice? Because in the Mass the same Jesus Christ who offered Himself on Calvary now offers Himself on the altar. The Priest is the same, the Victim is the same, and the end or purpose is the same.

The Priest is the same Jesus Christ whose sacred person the ordained priest represents and in whose Name he offers the Eucharistic Sacrifice.

The Victim is the same, namely the Savior in His human nature, with His true Body and Blood, and His human free will. Only the manner of offering is different. On the Cross, the sacrifice was bloody; in the Mass it is unbloody because Christ is now in His glorified state. But the heart of sacrifice is the voluntary, total offering of oneself to God. Christ makes this voluntary offering in every Mass, signified by the separate consecration of the bread and wine into the Body and Blood of the Redeemer.

The end or purpose is the same, namely to give glory to God, to thank Him, to obtain His mercy, and to ask Him for our needs. But, as we have seen, whereas on Calvary Christ merited our salvation, it is mainly through the Mass that He now dispenses the riches of His saving grace.

Eucharist as Communion-Sacrament

The biblical foundation for Holy Communion is what Christ Himself did at the Last Supper. As narrated by St. Matthew, Jesus first offered the apostles what He was about to change, then changed the bread and wine, and then gave them Communion.

> And while they were at supper, Jesus took bread and blessed and broke and gave it to His disciples and said, "Take you and eat, this is my Body." And taking the chalice He gave thanks and gave it to them saying, "Drink you all of this. For this is my Blood of the New Testament which shall be shed for many unto remission of sins" (Matthew 26:26–28).

St. John, who does not give us the narrative of the institution of the Eucharist, devotes a whole chapter to Christ's promise of giving His followers His own flesh to eat and His own blood to drink.

What Christ emphasizes is the absolute necessity of being nourished by His Body and Blood if the supernatural life received at Baptism is to be sustained.

> I tell you most solemnly, if you do not eat the flesh of the Son of Man and drink His blood, you will not have life in you. Anyone who does eat my flesh and drink my blood has eternal life and I shall raise him up on the last day. For my flesh is real food and my blood is real drink. He who eats my flesh and drinks my blood lives in me and I live in Him. As I, who am sent by the living Father, myself draw life from the Father, so whoever eats me will draw life from me. This is the bread come down from heaven; not like the bread our ancestors ate. They are dead, but anyone who eats this bread will live forever (John 6: 53–58).

Throughout the gospels and St. Paul, Christ uses words like "take," "eat," "drink," always clearly indicating that the Eucharist is to be taken into the mouth and consumed. No less, and far more, than material food and drink are necessary to sustain the natural life of the body, so Holy Communion must be received to support and nourish the supernatural life of the soul.

Effects of Holy Communion. Since the earliest times, the benefits of receiving the Body and Blood of Christ were spelled out to encourage frequent, even daily, Holy Communion.

Thus, St. Cyril of Jerusalem (died 387) said that

reception of the Eucharist makes the Christian a "Christbearer" and "one body and one blood with Him" (*Catecheses*, 4,3). St. John Chrysostom (died 407) speaks of a mixing of the Body of Christ with our body, ". . . in order to show the great love that He has for us. He mixed Himself with us, and joined His Body with us, so that we might become one like a bread connected with the body" (*Homily* 46,3). These and other comparisons of how Communion unites the recipient with Christ are based on Christ's own teaching, and St. Paul's statement that, "the bread which we break, is it not the partaking of the Body of the Lord? For we, being many, are one bread, all that partake of this bread" (I Corinthians 10:16–17).

So, too, the Church officially teaches that "Every effect which bodily food and bodily drink produce in our corporeal life, by preserving this life, increasing this life, healing this life, and satisfying this life—is also produced by this Sacrament in the spiritual life" (Council of Florence, November 22, 1439). Thus:

1. Holy Communion preserves the supernatural life of the soul by giving the communicant supernatural strength to resist temptation, and by weakening the power of concupiscence. It reinforces the ability of our free will to withstand the assaults of the devil. In a formal definition, the Church calls Holy Communion "an antidote by which we are preserved from grievous sins" (Council of Trent, October 11, 1551).

2. Holy Communion increases the life of grace already present by vitalizing our supernatural life and strengthening the virtues and gifts of the Holy Spirit we possess. To be emphasized, however, is that the main effect of Communion is not to remit sin. In fact, a person in conscious mortal sin commits a sacrilege by going to Communion.

3. Holy Communion cures the spiritual diseases of the soul by cleansing it of venial sins and the temporal punishment due to sin. No less than serving as an antidote to protect the soul from mortal sins, Communion is "an antidote by which we are freed from our daily venial sins" (Council of Trent, October 11, 1551). The remission of venial sins and of the temporal sufferings due to sin takes place immediately by reason of the acts of perfect love of God, which are awakened by the reception of the Eucharist. The extent of this remission depends on the intensity of our charity when receiving Communion.

4. Holy Communion gives us a spiritual joy in the service of Christ, in defending His cause, in performing the duties of our state of life, and in making the sacrifices required of us in imitating the life of our Savior.

On Christ's own promise, Holy Communion is a pledge of heavenly glory and of our bodily resurrection from the dead (John 6:55). St. Irenaeus (died 202) simply declared that, "when our bodies partake of the Eucharist, they are no longer corruptible as they have the hope of eternal resurrection" (*Against the Heresies*, IV, 18,5).

Reception of the Eucharist. We may distinguish four stages in the Church's history on the frequency of receiving Holy Communion. In the early centuries, the Eucharist was received often, even daily. By the early Middle Ages, neglect of the Sacrament caused a general council of the Church to pass a law that is still in effect. The Fourth Lateran Council in 1215 A.D. decreed that on reaching the age of discretion, every Catholic should receive Holy Communion after having gone to the Sacrament of Penance.

In the sixteenth century, the Council of Trent repeated the foregoing decree and condemned "anyone who denies that each and every one of Christ's faithful of both sexes is bound, when he reaches the age of reason, to receive Communion at least every year during the Paschal season according to the command of holy Mother Church" (October 11, 1551).

With the rise of Jansenism in the seventeenth century, reception of Communion reached an all-time low. One result was that people were known not to make their First Communion until they were dying. All the while, however, zealous apostles of the Eucharist, like Saints Ignatius Loyola, Vincent de Paul and Alphonsus Liguori, were urging the faithful to receive as often as possible. In his *Spiritual Exercises*, St. Ignatius says, we should "praise the reception of the Most Holy Sacrament once a year, and what is much better once a month, and much better still every eight days, always with the requisite and due dispositions" (*Rules for Thinking with the Church*, 3).

Finally in 1905, Pope St. Pius X issued his famous decree on frequent communion, and it has made Eucharistic history. The pope said:

> Frequent and daily Communion, as a thing most earnestly desired by Christ our Lord and by the Catholic Church, should be open to all the faithful of whatever rank and condition of life; so that no one who is in the state of grace, and who approaches the holy table with a right and devout intention, can lawfully be hindered from receiving. . . .
>
> A right intention consists in this: that he who approaches the holy table should do so, not out of routine or vainglory or human respect, but for the purpose of pleasing God, of being more closely united with Him by charity, and of seeking this divine remedy for his weaknesses and defects (December 20, 1905).

The new Code of Canon Law builds on this legislation of St. Pius X and even permits reception twice a day. According to the Code, "A person who has received the Most Holy Eucharist may receive it again on the same day only within a Eucharistic celebration in which that person participates" (Canon 917).

Eucharist as Presence-Sacrament

Although we have reserved our reflections on the Real Presence for the end, we could just as well have begun with the Eucharist as Presence-Sacrament. The reason is that logically, the Mass and Holy Communion derive all their meaning from the Real Presence of Jesus Christ in the Blessed Sacrament.

As we did before, so here again we shall draw on the irreversible teaching of the Council of Trent about the Real Presence. The original doctrine is worded in the form of anathemas. What follows is a summary list of these dogmas expressed in positive terms.

1. The Body and Blood of Christ together with the soul and divinity of Christ and therefore the whole Christ, is truly, really, and substantially contained in the sacrament of the most Holy Eucharist.

2. By that wonderful and extraordinary change, called transubstantiation, the whole substance of the bread is changed into Christ's Body, and the whole substance of the wine is changed into His Blood, so that only the species' properties of bread and wine remain.

3. In the venerable sacrament of the Eucharist, the whole Christ is contained under each species, and under each and every portion of either species when it is divided up.

4. After the consecration, the Body and Blood of our Lord Jesus Christ are present in the marvelous sacrament of the Eucharist. They are present not only in the use of the sacrament while it is being received, but also before and after. Consequently, the true Body and Blood of the Lord remain in the consecrated hosts or particles that are kept or left over after Communion.

5. Christ, the only-begotten Son of God, is to be adored in the holy sacrament of the Eucharist with the worship due to God and including external worship. The Blessed Sacrament is therefore to be honored with extraordinary festive celebrations, solemnly carried from place to place in processions, and is to be publicly exposed for the people's adoration.

6. The Holy Eucharist is to be kept in a sacred place (Council of Trent, October 11, 1551).

It is impossible to exaggerate the importance of the foregoing definitions of the Catholic Church on the Real Presence. No doubt, their doctrinal substance had been part of the Church's faith since the time of Christ. But the clear and simple expression of this faith in the sixteenth century marked a turning point in Catholic devotions to Jesus Christ, now present on earth no less than He was visibly present in first-century Palestine.

Transubstantiation. To identify what takes place in the consecration at Mass, the Church has come to employ the term "transubstantiation" (*trans* = change, *substantiation* = of substance). Because of its importance for understanding the Real Presence, this term deserves some explanation.

There are two kinds of changes which things can naturally undergo. They are called accidental and substantial changes. In an accidental change, something remains substantially the same, but its accidental or non-essential properties are transformed. Thus when a block of marble is carved into a statue, the marble remains marble, but its shape and form are changed.

In a substantial change, the former substance ceases to exist and becomes something else. Thus, when food is eaten, its substance is changed; it becomes part of the organism which consumes the food.

In transubstantiation there is a unique substantial change. The essence or substance of bread and wine ceases to exist, while the accidents or sensibly perceptible properties of bread and wine remain. This kind of change has no counterpart in nature; it belongs to the supernatural order.

What actually occurs? The substance of what was bread and wine is replaced by the living Christ. Although the external qualities of bread and wine remain, their substance is no longer on the altar. It is now the whole Christ, divinity and humanity, soul and body, and all the bodily qualities that make Christ, Christ.

In his historic encyclical *The Mystery of Faith*, Paul VI goes into great detail to show that transubstantiation produces a unique presence of Jesus

Christ on earth. The pope analyzes six ways in which the Savior is present and active in the world of human beings, but they are not the Real Presence. The Real Presence is unique because "it contains Christ Himself." Moreover, this presence is called *Real* because it is the presence "by which Christ, the God-Man is wholly and entirely present" (*Mysterium Fidei*, September 3, 1965).

Worship of the Holy Eucharist. There has been a remarkable development of doctrine on the Real Presence. Already in the infant Church, the faithful did not doubt that by the words of consecration by the priest, what had been bread is now the living Christ. However, as certain theories began to emerge that called the Real Presence into question, two things happened. The Church's magisterium began to express her Eucharistic faith in even sharper and clearer terms; and the Church's saints began to foster devotion to the living Christ who is present in our midst in the Blessed Sacrament.

The classic expression of faith in the Real Presence was drafted by Pope Gregory VII in a Eucharistic Creed that leaves no room for compromise.

I believe in my heart and openly profess that the bread and wine placed upon the altar are, by the mystery of the sacred prayer and the words of the Redeemer, substantially changed into the true and life-giving flesh and blood of Jesus Christ our Lord, and that after the consecration there is present the true body of Christ which was born of the Virgin and offered up for the salvation of the world, being hung on the cross and now sits at the right hand of the Father, and there is present the true blood of Christ which flowed from His side. They are present not only by means of a sign and of the efficacy of the sacrament, but also in the very reality and truth of their nature and substance (Council of Rome, February 11, 1079).

Long before this famous profession of faith, the Holy Eucharist had been worshipped by the faithful. But the adoration of the Real Presence for prolonged periods of time did not become widespread until about the beginning of the thirteenth century. The immediate occasion for this practice was the great devotion to the Blessed Sacrament of the Belgian Augustinian nun, St. Juliana of Mont Cornillon (1193–1258).

St. Juliana urged the bishop of Liege to institute a feast in honor of the Real Presence. The bishop ordered such a feast for his diocese in 1246. On September 8, 1264, the Belgian Pope, Urban IV, established the feast of Corpus Christi and ordered St. Thomas Aquinas to compose its Divine Office. Three of our best known Eucharistic hymns are part of this Divine Office, namely *Pange Lingua*, which closes with the two verses of *Tantum Ergo; Sacris Solemniis*, which closes with the two verses of *Panis Angelicus;* and *Verbum Supernum*, which closes with the two verses of *O Salutaris Hostia*.

No less than eleven canons of the new Code of Canon Law deal with "the Reservation and Veneration of the Most Holy Eucharist." They cover every significant aspect of Catholic veneration of the Holy Eucharist.

- The Sacrament is to be reserved in every cathedral, parish church and church or oratory of a religious institute or society of apostolic life (Canon 934).

- The church should be open to the faithful, "at least some hours each day so that they are able to spend some time in prayer before the Most Blessed Sacrament" (Canon 937).

- The tabernacle in which the Most Holy Eucharist is reserved should be situated in a distinguished place in the church or oratory, a place which is conspicuous, suitably adorned, and conducive to prayer" (Canon 938).

In one country after another, adoration of the Holy Eucharist has developed beyond anything seen in previous generations. Groups have been formed among the laity for this purpose. Some are local organizations associated with a single parish church or public oratory. Others reach out across the nation and even to other countries. Their common denominator is an intense desire to profess one's faith in Christ's Real Presence in the Eucharist, and to pray for the desperate help that people need in today's convulsive society.

Modern popes have not only supported this renewed devotion to the Eucharist, but have done all

they could to set the example for bishops to follow.
Thus Pope John Paul II established the daily exposition of the Blessed Sacrament in St. Peter's Basilica.
Every day, Monday through Friday, the Blessed Sacrament has been exposed all day, from Latin Mass in
the morning until Italian Vespers in the evening.
Two Sisters are in adoration in the Blessed Sacrament Chapel in St. Peter's. Pilgrims to Rome join in
their prayers before the Holy Eucharist.

When the Perpetual Eucharistic Exposition
opened, Pope John Paul II composed a prayer of
which the following are significant quotations.

Lord, "stay with us."

These words were spoken for the first time by
the disciples at Emmaus. In the course of the
centuries, they have been spoken infinite times,
by the lips of so many of your disciples and confessors, O Christ.

As Bishop of Rome and first servant of this
temple, which stands on the place of St. Peter's
martyrdom, I speak the same words today.

Stay! That we may meet you in prayer of adoration and thanksgiving, in prayer of expiation
and petition, to which all those who visit this basilica are invited.

Stay! You who are at one and the same time
veiled in the Eucharistic mystery of faith, and
also revealed under the species of bread and wine,
which you have assumed in this Sacrament.

The Eucharist is at the same time a constant
announcement of your second coming and the

sign of the final Advent, and also of the expectation of the whole Church.

Every day and every hour we wish to adore you, veiled under the species of bread and wine, to renew hope of the "call to glory" which you began with your glorified body "at the Father's right hand."

May the unworthy successor of Peter in the Roman See—and all those who take part in the adoration of your Eucharistic Presence—attest with every visit of theirs, and make ring out again the truth contained in the apostle's words: "Lord, you know everything; you know that I love you." Amen.

In one diocese after another, bishops have encouraged the adoration of Jesus Christ in the Blessed Sacrament by the faithful. In a world that is groping in darkness, the Church is telling people that Christ, "the light of the world" and "the power of salvation" is on earth to teach us and strengthen us on the road to heaven. All we need is to believe that He *is* here and ready to provide us with what we need.

PENANCE

As Catholics, we have no doubt that Christ instituted the sacrament of Penance on Easter Sunday night. St. John describes the event in great detail.

> In the evening of that same day, the first day of the week, the doors were closed in the room where the disciples were for fear of the Jews. Jesus came and stood among them. He said to them, "Peace be with you," and showed them His hands and His side. The disciples were filled with joy when they saw the Lord and He said to them again, "Peace be with you. As the Father sent me, so I am sending you." After saying this, He breathed on them and said, "Receive the Holy Spirit. For those whose sins you forgive, they are forgiven, for those whose sins you retain, they are retained" (John 20:19–23).

As we examine this narrative in the gospels, we notice a number of striking features. It was Christ's first appearance to the assembled disciples since His resurrection from the dead. To quiet their fears, Jesus told the frightened apostles, "Peace be with you." In doing this, He gave what He was about to institute its first name, the sacrament of peace. It was to reconcile a sinner and therefore restore peace between man and an offended God. Its effect was also to remove guilt from a sinful soul and therefore give peace within a man's heart. Why? Because the most fundamental cause of all disturbance of soul and the absence of peace is the sense of guilt. The final effect of this sacrament was to restore harmony in a society injured or destroyed by enmity, greed, and injustice, and therefore produce peace between people in the community in which they live.

Moreover, Jesus told the apostles He was sending them as the Father had sent Him. The Father had sent the Son as the merciful Savior of sinners. In fact, that is what the name *Jesus* means, "the One who saves." Saves from sin. In like manner, the apostles and their successors, the bishops and priests of the Catholic church, are being sent among sinful people as ministers of God's mercy to bring them the threefold peace which is lost by sin.

As Christ spoke to the apostles, He breathed on them and said, "Receive the Holy Spirit." It is by divine power that priests are empowered to forgive sins. Even as sin estranges a soul from God, so its forgiveness restores the soul's friendship with God which is holiness.

Teaching of the Church

In the course of her history, the Catholic Church has many times been required to defend and explain her faith in the sacrament of Penance. However, as with so many other revealed truths, the most elaborate doctrinal exposition of the sacrament of Penance was made by the Council of Trent. Its principal defined dogmas cover every aspect of this sacrament of God's mercy.

1.   Penance is truly and properly a sacrament instituted by Christ our Lord to reconcile the faithful with God Himself as often as they fall into sin after baptism.

2.   Christ's words to the apostles, "Whose sins you shall forgive, they are forgiven them; and whose sins you shall retain, they are retained" have, from the beginning, been understood by the Church to refer to the power of remitting and of retaining sins in the sacrament of Penance.

3.   In the sacrament of Penance, three acts are required of the penitent, namely, contrition, confession, and satisfaction.

4.   To receive forgiveness in this sacrament it is sufficient to be sorry because a person realizes the seriousness of his sins and fears the loss of eternal happiness and the pains of eternal damnation, and resolves to lead a better life.

169

5. Sacramental confession was instituted by divine law and is necessary for salvation by the same divine law. Moreover, the Church's teaching on confessing one's sins secretly to a priest alone is not of human origin, but goes back to the beginning to the command of Christ.

6. According to divine law, it is necessary to confess each and every mortal sin, even secret sins against the last two commandments of God. Moreover, it is necessary to confess the circumstances which change the nature of a sin.

7. Sacramental absolution by the priest is a judicial act and not merely a declaring that a person's sins are forgiven. Thus the confession by the penitent is necessary so that the priest can give him absolution.

8. Priests are the only ones who can give absolution.

9. God does not always remit all the punishment at the same time that he remits our sins.

10. Satisfaction for the temporal punishment due to sins can be made to God by the trials sent by God and patiently endured, by the penances imposed by the priest in confession, by penances voluntarily undertaken such as fasts, prayers, almsgiving, and other works of piety.

11. The satisfaction by which penitents atone for their sins through Jesus Christ is a true worship of God.

12. Even after the eternal punishment is taken

away by sacramental absolution, temporal punishment normally remains to be expiated.

Confession of Sins

It may be surprising that Christ's institution of the sacrament of Penance was not seriously challenged until the late Middle Ages.

Typical of the Church's tradition are the liturgical texts for the ordination of bishops. One formula of episcopal ordination dating from the latter half of the fourth century, offers this prayer to God.

> Grant him, O Lord Almighty, by Thy Christ, the fullness of Thy Spirit, that he may have the power to pardon sin, in accordance with Thy command, that he may loose every bond which binds the sinner by reason of that power which Thou hast granted to Thy apostles (*Apostolic Constitutions*, 8,5,7).

Equally typical was the Church's belief that in order to obtain remission of sins, a person had to confess to the bishop or priest. In the mid-fifth century, an abuse had crept in which took papal intervention to stop. Pope Leo I, writing to a group of bishops in Italy, says:

> I have recently learned that some are presuming to act against a rule set down from apostolic times. I decree that the practice they have bra-

zenly introduced be completely stopped. I refer to the fact that penitents are told they must publicly recite each one of their sins, which they had previously set down in writing. It is sufficient that the sins which burden a person's conscience should be secretly confessed only to priests (*Letter to the Bishops of Campania,* 168,2).

Confession of sins was therefore presumed. The pope was simply correcting a rigorist interpretation of what he called an apostolic practice, namely the private confession of one's sins to a priest.

By the early fifteenth century, partly due to the lax morality of some of the clergy, the idea arose that an immoral priest or bishop could not give absolution. In fact, a general council of the Church had to be called to decide that internal sorrow for sin was not sufficient to be reconciled with God. Moreover, the council declared "in order to be saved, a Christian has the obligation, over and above heartfelt contrition, of confessing to a priest when a qualified one is available, and only to a priest, not to lay person or persons, no matter how good and devout the latter may be" (Council of Constance, February 22, 1418).

A century later the Council of Trent defined in great detail, as we have seen, the necessity of what has come to be called auricular confession of sins in the sacrament of Penance.

The new Code of Canon Law restates this doctrine in clear terms.

Individual and integral confession and absolution constitute the sole ordinary means by which a member of the faithful who is conscious of grave sin is reconciled with God and with the Church (Canon 960).

Since the first Code of Canon Law was published in 1917, questions had been raised about the validity of general absolution. On several occasions, the Holy See had been asked under what conditions sacramental absolution could be given to many at the same time. The cases applied to situations where there was either no priest or a priest could not stay long enough to hear the confessions of all the penitents. Such too would be the case of absolving soldiers when a battle was imminent or in progress. The same would hold true for civilians and soldiers in danger of death during a hostile invasion. Rome's decisions on such cases prompted the provision in the new Code of Canon Law which states that, "General absolution, without prior individual confession cannot be given to a number of penitents together unless:

- danger of death threatens and there is not time for the priest or priests to hear the confessions of the individual penitents,

- there exists a grave necessity . . . so that without fault of their own the penitents are deprived of the sacramental grace of Holy Communion for a lengthy period of time. A sufficient necessity is not, however, considered to exist when confessors cannot be available merely because of a great gathering of penitents, such as can occur on some major feast day or pilgrimage" (Canon 961).

There is one more condition which the Church sets down for valid general absolution. "For a member of Christ's faithful," says the Code, "to benefit validly from a sacramental absolution given to a number of people simultaneously, it is required not only that he or she be properly disposed, but be also at the same time personally resolved to confess in due time each of the grave sins which cannot for the moment be thus confessed" (Canon 962). Accordingly, Christ's precept of making a personal confession of mortal sins remains even when for exceptional reasons, general absolution had been received.

The Code of Canon Law also repeats what by now is a centuries-old prescription regarding first confession. It occurs in conjunction with the precept on first Holy Communion.

It is primarily the duty of priests and of those who take their place, as it is the duty of the parish priest, to ensure that children who have reached the use of reason are properly prepared and, having made their sacramental confession, are nourished by this divine food as soon as possible (Canon 914).

Absolutely speaking, by divine law, the sacrament of Penance must be received before a person in mortal sin may receive Holy Communion. By ecclesiastical law, "All the faithful who have reached the age of discretion are bound faithfully to confess their grave sins at least once a year" (Canon 989).

However, "the faithful are recommended to confess also their venial sins" (Canon 988). In fact, one of the true developments of doctrine in modern times has been the growing realization of the great value of frequent confession, even when no mortal sins are to be confessed. It is true that venial sins can be forgiven in other ways, but frequent sacramental confession has values that have been proved by long experience.

> By it genuine self-knowledge is increased, Christian humility grows, bad habits are corrected, spiritual neglect and tepidity are resisted, the conscience is purified, the will strengthened, a voluntary self-control is attained, and grace is increased in virtue of the sacrament itself (Pope Pius XII, *The Mystical Body of Christ*, 88).

Those who have cultivated the habit of receiving the sacrament of Penance often, on a regular basis, testify to the truth of this teaching of the Church. It is all the more necessary in a world that has become so oblivious of the evil of offending an all-loving God.

Anointing of the Sick

The sacrament of Anointing of the Sick was already implied in Christ's first mission to the twelve apostles. "So they set off to preach repentance; and they cast out many devils, and anointed many sick people with oil and cured them" (Mark 6:13).

Some time during His public ministry, Christ personally instituted anointing "as a true and proper sacrament of the New Testament" (Council of Trent, November 25, 1551). After the Lord's ascension into heaven, anointing was commended to the faithful and promulgated by the Apostle James, "the brother of the Lord." What St. James says is that the sick should be anointed. He also declares who is to perform the anointing and what effects are to be expected from the conferring of this sacrament:

> If one of you is ill he should send for the elders of the Church, and they must anoint him with oil in the name of the Lord, and pray over him.
>
> The prayer of faith will save the sick man and

the Lord will raise him up again; and if he be in sin, they shall be forgiven him (James 5:14–15).

Among the few passages of Scripture that the Church has officially (and infallibly) defined are these two verses in the letter of James the Younger, or Less, who was a near relative of our Lord. According to the Council of Trent (November 25, 1551) the elders to whom St. James refers are "priests ordained by the bishop."

Sacramental Ritual

Until the Second Vatican Council, the anointing had to be with olive oil blessed by the bishop. This is still the ordinary material used in the administration of this sacrament. But Pope Paul VI decided that since olive oil is unobtainable or difficult to obtain in some parts of the world, in the future any oil "obtained from plants" could be used.

Moreover, in keeping with the directives of the Council, the ritual was simplified. The formal papal declaration deserves to be fully quoted:

> The Sacrament of the Anointing of the Sick is administered to those who are dangerously ill, by anointing them on the forehead and hands with olive oil, or if opportune, with another vegetable oil properly blessed, and saying once only the following words: "Through this holy anointing and His most loving mercy, may the Lord

assist you by the grace of the Holy Spirit, so that freed from your sins, He may save you and in His goodness raise you up" (*Apostolic Constitution on the Sacrament of Anointing of the Sick*, November 30, 1972).

In case of necessity, it is sufficient that a single anointing be given on the forehead. In fact, if the particular condition of the sick person warrants it, another suitable part of the body may be anointed, while pronouncing the whole formula.

The sacrament can be repeated under two circumstances:

- If the sick person, having been once anointed, recovers and then falls sick again.
- If in the course of the same sickness, the danger becomes more serious.

According to the directives of Canon Law, "the Anointing of the Sick can be administered to any member of the faithful who, having reached the age of reason, begins to be in danger due to sickness or old age" (Canon 1004).

As explained by Paul VI, "Extreme Unction, which may also and more fittingly be called 'Anointing of the Sick' is not a sacrament for those only who are at the point of death. Consequently, as soon as any one of the faithful begins to be in danger of death from sickness or old age, the appropriate time to receive this sacrament has certainly already arrived" (*Apostolic Constitution*). The key words are "begins to be in danger," as contrasted with "at the point of death."

The new Code is also more lenient than the former regarding doubtful cases. "If there is any doubt," the law now says, "as to whether the sick person has reached the use of reason, or is dangerously ill, or is dead, this sacrament is to be administered" (Canon 1005). This is a change from the former prescription that the sacrament "is to be administered conditionally."

Two further provisions exist in the Church's general law. One concerns the kind of desire a person must have to receive anointing, and the other concerns people who are living in notorious sin. On the one hand, therefore, "this sacrament is to be administered to the sick who, when they were in possession of their faculties, at least implicitly asked for it" (Canon 1006). On the other hand, "the Anointing of the Sick is not to be conferred upon those who obstinately persist in a manifestly grave sin" (Canon 1007). Between these two situations lies the whole issue of having the proper dispositions to receive the graces available through anointing.

Spiritual and Bodily Effects

The Church explains the words of St. James about the effect of anointing by distinguishing two kinds of blessing which this sacrament confers. The principal blessing is for the soul, the secondary is for the body.

How is the soul blessed by the Holy Spirit through anointing? In several ways:

1. The guilt of mortal sin is removed, so that a sinner is restored to God's friendship. With the guilt the eternal punishment due to mortal sin is also removed. On this level, anointing has the same effect as Baptism and the sacrament of Penance. Moreover, the sorrow required for remission of sin is the fear of God, based on faith, which makes anointing so precious. Even though a person is unconscious when anointed, yet he is restored to God's grace with the minimum requirement of what we call imperfect contrition, which means sorrow for sin because a believer fears the just punishments of an offended God.

2. Also, the guilt and temporal punishment of venial sins are removed, depending on the dispositions of the person anointed.

3. Temporal punishment still due to forgiven sins is removed, again depending on the spiritual dispositions with which the sacrament of anointing is received.

4. Anointing strengthens the sick person in especially two ways:

• Trust in God's mercy is deepened by reassuring the one anointed that, no matter how deeply God had been offended, He is a loving God who wants only the salvation of the sinner.

- Courage is received to face the future, especially the prospect of death. A person is prepared to enter eternity with a peaceful acceptance of God's will.

5. Anointing gives extraordinary patience in enduring whatever sufferings are experienced, and enables the one anointed to resist the temptations of the devil to discouragement or even despair.

The Church's teaching on the bodily effects of the sacrament is simply expressed. "This anointing," says the Council of Trent, "occasionally restores health to the body if health would be an advantage to the salvation of the soul." In other words, the spiritual effects of anointing are unconditional provided the sick person is properly disposed. But the benefits to the body, including restoration to health, depends on God's foreknowledge of whether this would be good for the soul. Sickness is not an absolute evil. If God foresees that being healed in body is for our supernatural good, He will "raise us up" physically so that we might also be "raised up" spiritually and be more assured of our eternal destiny.

HOLY ORDERS

Among the sacraments, none is more distinctively Catholic than the sacrament of Order. The plural, Orders, is commonly used because there are three levels of this one sacrament, namely the diaconate, priesthood, and episcopate.

In the Church's own language, this sacrament is described in the new Code of Canon Law.

> By divine institution, some among Christ's faithful are, through the sacrament of Order, marked with an indelible character, and are thus constituted sacred ministers. . . .
>
> They are thereby consecrated and deputed so that each according to his own grade, they fulfill, in the person of Christ the Head, the offices of teaching, sanctifying, and ruling, and so they nourish the people of God (Canon 1008).

All three levels of this sacrament are conferred by the imposition of hands and the appropriate prayer of consecration. Only bishops can confer the sacrament of Order.

Only a baptized man can validly receive the sacrament of Order (Canon 1024). This rests on positive divine law. Christ called only men to be His apostles. According to the testimony of Sacred Scripture and the unchangeable practice of the Church, the hierarchical powers were conferred only on men.

Episcopate

The episcopate is the highest form of the sacrament of Orders. Thus the Council of Trent defined that bishops are superior to priests.

This pre-eminence of the bishops refers both to their exercise of authority and to their power of consecration. But their authority depends on their own consecration. Thus only bishops have the power of ordaining bishops, priests, or deacons. The common teaching is that the difference between bishops and priests (presbyters) existed from the beginning of the Church through a direct institution by Christ.

"No bishop is permitted to consecrate anyone as bishop unless it is first established that a pontifical mandate has been issued" (Canon 1013). This means that a priest may not be consecrated a bishop unless it is clearly proved that the one to be consecrated has been officially approved by the Holy See for episcopal consecration.

As understood by Christ, the divine mission which He first entrusted to the apostles was to last until the end of time. That is why the apostles were careful to appoint successors in this hierarchical society.

By the laying on of hands these men were ordained to the episcopate so that by the year 100 A.D., there were over one hundred dioceses in existence around the Mediterranean world.

In every case, the ordination to the episcopate began with the apostles ordained by Christ at the Last Supper, so that the episcopal succession of bishops can be literally called the apostolic succession. Every validly ordained bishop in the world today can trace his ordination historically to that first ordination on Holy Thursday night.

What needs to be emphasized is that the power of episcopal orders is also the foundation of episcopal authority. The Second Vatican Council could not be clearer:

> That divine mission, which was committed by Christ to the apostles, is destined to last until the end of the world (Matthew 28:20), since the gospel which they are charged to hand on, is for the Church, the principle of all its life until the end of time. For that very reason, the apostles were careful to appoint successors in this hierarchically constituted society. . . .
>
> They accordingly designated such men and made the ruling that likewise on their death other proven men should take over their ministry. . . .
>
> Thus according to the testimony of St. Irenaeus, the apostolic tradition is manifested and

184

preserved in the whole world by those who were made bishops by the apostles and by their successors down to our own time (*Constitution on the Church*, III, 20).

The apostolic succession of the bishops is reflected in the prayer of consecration by which priests are ordained to the episcopate. The ordaining prelate, after laying hands on the one to be made bishop, prays: "Now pour out upon this chosen one that power which flows from you, that perfect Spirit which He gave to the apostles, who established the Church in every place as the sanctuary where your name would always be praised and glorified."

In virtue of their ordination, bishops receive the fullness of the sacrament of Order. Only they can confer this sacrament on others. But, as we have seen, their power to teach and rule the People of God depends on their approval by the Bishop of Rome.

Priesthood

In the New Testament, only bishops and priests possess priestly powers. In the Church's language, bishops have the fullness of the priesthood, "the highest priest of the first order." Presbyters (priests) are "simple priests of the second order."

Challenged on the priesthood, the Catholic Church has more than once defended her teaching as revealed by God and therefore the irreversible truth.

The most explicit doctrine was taught by the Council of Trent.

1. There is a visible and external priesthood in the New Testament. It consists in the power of consecrating and offering the Body and Blood of the Lord, and of remitting and of retaining sins. The priesthood, therefore, is not only an office and simple ministry of preaching.

2. Orders, or holy ordination, is truly and properly a sacrament instituted by Christ our Lord.

3. There is a divinely instituted hierarchy consisting of bishops, priests, and ministers.

4. Bishops are superior to priests and have power to confirm and ordain. The power they have is not common to both them and to priests. Moreover, the orders conferred by them do not depend on the call or consent of the people, nor of the secular power (Council of Trent, July 15, 1563).

Building on these principles of doctrine, the Second Vatican Council stressed the need for priests to cooperate with the bishops. Together with their bishop, priests form a unique priestly community, although dedicated to a variety of different duties. In each local assembly of the faithful, priests may be said to represent the bishop with whom they are to be associated in all trust and generosity (*Constitution of the Church*, III, 28).

186

Diaconate

The name *deacon* means "servant" or "minister" and it is used in this sense in the Scriptures. Yet the constant tradition of the Catholic Church recognizes the office of deacon as a divine institution. The narrative of the martyrdom of St. Stephen (Acts 6:1–6) describes the first beginnings of this office.

Among the duties of deacons in the first centuries of the Church, the following stand out. They were stewards of the Church's funds, and of the alms collected for widows and orphans; they were to help with the care of the poor and the aged; their special duty was to read the gospel; they would also preach to the people; they were especially to bring the Holy Eucharist to the sick in their homes; confer the sacrament of Baptism, and assist the bishop or priest in the celebration of the Eucharistic Liturgy.

The exercise of the diaconate enabled those who were to become priests to prepare themselves for their priestly life. But as time went on, there was a gradual decrease in the number of those who wished to remain deacons all their lives, without going on to the priesthood. As a result, the permanent diaconate almost entirely disappeared in the Latin Rite of the Catholic Church.

The Council of Trent proposed the idea of restoring the permanent diaconate. Gradually this idea matured, and the Second Vatican Council officially supported the desire of those bishops who wanted permanent deacons to be ordained "where such would lead to the good of souls."

One provision of the Code of Canon Law recognizes that married men may become permanent deacons: "A candidate for the permanent diaconate who is not married may be admitted to the diaconate only when he has completed at least his twenty-fifth year. If he is married, not until he has completed at least his thirty-fifth year, and then with the consent of his wife" (Canon 1031, 2). According to the Church's tradition, a married deacon who has lost his wife cannot enter a new marriage (Pope Paul VI, *Norms for the Order of Diaconate*, 6).

However, "A candidate for the permanent diaconate who is not married, and likewise a candidate for the priesthood, is not to be admitted to the order of diaconate unless he has, in the prescribed rite, publicly before God and the Church undertaken the obligation of celibacy, or unless he has taken perpetual vows in a religious institute" (Canon 1037).

Second Vatican Council

In its *Constitution on the Liturgy*, the Second Vatican Council pointed out that, "the liturgy is made up of unchangeable elements divinely instituted and of elements subject to changes" (21). One result was that the centuries-old distinction was dropped between major and minor orders. The major orders were the episcopate, priesthood, diaconate, and subdiaconate. The minor orders were acolyte, porter, lector, and exorcist. Since the subdiaconate was not a sacrament, Paul VI suppressed the subdiaconate in the Latin Rite of the Catholic Church.

Two of the minor orders, acolyte and lector, became simple ministries. Only men can assume these ministries. According to Canon Law, "Lay men whose age and talents meet the requirements prescribed by decree of the Episcopal Conference, can be given the stable ministry of lector and of acolyte through the prescribed liturgical rite" (Canon 230).

Among the duties of the acolyte are:

1.   To assist the deacon and to minister to the priest in the liturgy, especially at Mass.

2.   To distribute Holy Communion as an extraordinary minister, whenever priests or deacons are unable to do so or the number of communicants is so large that the Holy Sacrifice would be unduly prolonged.

3.   To expose the Blessed Sacrament for the veneration of the faithful, but not to give Benediction.

4.   To instruct the faithful in their role at liturgical functions.

Correspondingly, among the duties of the ministry of lector are:

1.   To read the Scriptures at liturgical functions, but not the gospel.

2. To announce the intentions of the Prayer of the Faithful at Mass.

3. To direct the singing and participation of the faithful.

4. To instruct the faithful in the worthy reception of the sacraments (Pope Paul VI, *Certain Ministries*, August 15, 1972).

The minor order of "porter" had long become symbolic. Originally the porter not only took care of the church doors, but carried out the functions of the sexton or sacristan of a church. The modern custodian has replaced both porter and sexton.

So, too, the former minor order of "exorcist" has been absorbed in the priesthood. Exorcism is now classified among the sacramentals and covered by the Church's canon law.

No one may lawfully exorcise the possessed without the special and express permission of the local Ordinary. . . .

This permission is to be granted by the local Ordinary only to a priest endowed with piety, prudence, and integrity of life (Canon 1172).

One closing observation on the sacrament of Orders should be made. Not everyone has received the grace to be ordained. As St. Paul told the early Christians, "One does not take the honor upon himself, but he is called by God, just as Aaron was" (Hebrews 5:4). This is especially true of the priesthood, including its highest form in the episcopate. Christ Himself called only certain men to be apostles; so He continues to call those whom He wills. When they are ordained, it is from Him that they receive the principal powers of the priesthood: to consecrate and offer the Body and Blood of our Lord, and to forgive sins.

MARRIAGE

Marriage is not of human origin. It was instituted by God, as described in the opening chapters of the Book of Genesis.

But when Christ came into the world He elevated the natural institution to the level of a sacrament. He wished to provide not only individuals with the means they need, as persons, to reach eternal life: He also wanted to give grace to His followers as social beings. Marriage is the foundation of the family, which is the bedrock of human society.

In the Church's own language, the sacrament of Marriage is a contract indeed, but it is also a covenant.

The marriage covenant, by which a man and a woman establish between themselves a partnership of their whole life, and which of its own very nature is ordered to the well-being of the spouses and to the procreation and upbringing of children

192

has, between the baptized, been raised by Christ the Lord to the dignity of a sacrament.

Consequently, a valid marriage contract cannot exist between baptized persons without its being by that very fact a sacrament (Canon 1055).

The only condition, therefore, for a marriage to be a sacrament is that both husband and wife are baptized at the time they marry. This applies to all baptized persons, whether Catholic or not.

Essential Properties

Two properties of every marriage are unity and indissolubility. Both qualities acquire a distinctive firmness when the marriage is a sacrament.

Unity. By the unity of marriage the Catholic Church understands the monogamy of marriage. This means only one man is married to one woman. It therefore excludes polygamy, which literally means having more than one spouse at the same time (*poly* = many + *gamos* = marriage). Historically there have been two forms of polygamy practiced over the centuries. In polygyny a man has more than one wife at the same time (*poly* = many + *gyne* = woman). In polyandry a woman has more than one husband at the same time. Popular usage has practically identified polygamy with polygyny, although the two terms do not really mean the same thing.

Polyandry is the simultaneous marriage of one woman with two or more men (*poly* = many + *aner* = man). Historically less common than polygyny, it was often accompanied by female infanticide as a logical result of a marital system where there was a plurality of potential husbands.

Between the two forms of polygamy, polyandry was never permitted or even tolerated throughout the whole period of the Old Testament. Polygyny on the other hand was permitted for a certain time, as appears in the lives of such men as Abraham, Jacob, and David. But with the coming of Christ, polygamy was revoked. The Savior's language is very clear (Matthew 19:3–9; Mark 10:1–2; Luke 16:18).

In the sixteenth century, the Council of Trent condemned anyone who claimed that "Christians are permitted to have several wives simultaneously and that such a practice is not forbidden by any divine law" (November 11, 1563). In the twentieth century, the Church became more explicit. Not only is polygamy forbidden to Christians but, we are told, Christ wished "to condemn any form of polygamy or polyandry." In other words, since the rise of Christianity, polygamy and polyandry are forbidden to all human beings. The restoration of monogamy, which was originally universal, is itself also universal (Pope Pius XI, *Casti Connubii*, II).

Indissolubility. Practically speaking, what the Catholic Church had especially to defend was not so much simultaneous as successive polygamy. The main challenge to her defense of Christ's teaching was the claim that married people can divorce and remarry while their first spouse is still living.

In order to make her position absolutely clear, the Church distinguishes between what is called internal and what may be called external indissolubility.

Internal indissolubility means that a marriage cannot be dissolved from within. What unites a couple in marriage is a deeply interior bond of which God is the Author and which inseparably joins husband and wife before God, until death. It is Catholic doctrine that in a sacramental marriage, this bond is absolutely indissoluble. There have been several uncompromising, infallible pronouncements on this crucial area of Christian matrimony.

1. Christian marriage cannot be dissolved by reason of heresy, domestic incompatibility, or willful desertion by one of the parties.

2. The Church is not in error when she teaches, according to the doctrine of the gospels and apostles (Mark 10; I Corinthians 7) that the marriage bond cannot be dissolved because of adultery on the part of either the husband or the wife.

3. Consequently, neither party, not even the innocent one who gave no cause for the adultery, can contract another marriage while the other party is still living.

4. Adultery is therefore committed both by the husband who dismisses his adulterous wife and marries again, and by the wife who dismisses her

adulterous husband and marries again (Council of Trent, November 11, 1563).

In practice, the Church understands a marriage to be indissoluble by any human authority, civil or ecclesiastical, when three conditions are fulfilled:

- Both husband and wife were validly baptized before marriage.

- There has been a valid marriage contract, in which husband and wife knew they were entering a lifelong union which was open to the generation of children, and they both freely chose to enter this kind of marriage.

- There was natural, not contraceptive, intercourse after marriage.

Provided all three of these conditions were fulfilled, there can be no dissolution of the internal bond of such a marriage.

External, or outward indissolubility refers to "separation from bed and board or from cohabitation." Christ Himself provided for this when He told the Pharisees that, "whosoever shall put away his wife, except it be for fornication, and marries another, commits adultery" (Matthew 19:9). There are, therefore, grounds for a temporary or even permanent separation of husband and wife. But the Catholic Church believes that a sacramental and consummated marriage cannot be internally dissolved no matter how grave the reasons which may justify external separation of the spouses.

Pauline Privilege. Only a sacramental and consummated marriage is indissoluble by any human authority. What, then, is to be said about marriages that are not sacramental? The Church describes such marriages as held together by a "natural bond." A natural bond can be dissolved.

In general, two forms of non-sacramental marriages exist. Either one or both partners are not baptized when they marry. In both cases, no sacrament of marriage takes place.

The classic form of dissolving the natural bond is the Pauline Privilege. It is carefully expressed in the Code of Canon Law.

> In virtue of the Pauline Privilege, a marriage entered into by two unbaptized persons is dissolved in favor of the faith of the party who received baptism, by the very fact that a new marriage is contracted by that same party, provided the unbaptized party departs. . . .

> The unbaptized party is considered to depart if he or she is unwilling to live with the baptized party, or to live peacefully without offence to the Creator, unless the baptized party has, after the reception of Baptism, given the other just cause to depart (Canon 1143).

However, even a marriage between a baptized and a non-baptized person can be dissolved "in favor of the faith," also called "privilege of the faith." The circumstances would be similar to those of a Pauline Privilege, where one partner wishes to become Catholic but the non-Catholic spouse places grave obstacles to the practice of the Catholic faith.

The biblical grounds for the Pauline Privilege and the privilege of faith dissolution of the natural bond are in St. Paul (I Corinthians 7:12–16). Implied in both privileges is that only a valid sacramental and consummated marriage cannot be dissolved under any circumstances.

The Sacrament

Instituted by Christ to provide a lifetime flow of graces, Christian marriage is a sacrament which the marrying spouses confer on each other.

The bishop, priest, or deacon who assists at the marriage is a representative of the Church. He confirms the consent of marriage by the two partners and is an official witness to the marital contract, and the one who presides over the liturgical ceremony.

When a Catholic enters marriage with a non-Catholic, the Church must give a dispensation. One of the grounds for the dispensation is a formal statement made by the Catholic party. There are two parts to the agreement: "The Catholic party declares that he or she is prepared to remove dangers of falling away from the faith, and makes a sincere promise to do all in his or her power in order that all the children be baptized and brought up in the Catholic Church" (Canon 1125).

Since the Second Vatican Council, a dispensation can also be obtained for a Catholic to be married to a non-Catholic without having a bishop, priest, or deacon witness the marriage ceremony.

The Catholic Church claims to herself the sole and exclusive right to make laws and administer justice in the matrimonial affairs of baptized persons. Always understood is that the Church's jurisdiction applies to everything which belongs to the sacrament of Matrimony.

Historically this claim of the Church's rights over the sacrament of Marriage has been one of the main reasons for her periodic conflict with the State. The Church fully recognizes the rights of the State in purely temporal matters, but she insists that, because Christian marriage is a sacrament, Christ entrusted to the Church all final authority over marital morality.

The modern popes have repeatedly proclaimed the Church's authority over Christian marriage. They have seen the legalization of divorce and remarriage, of contraception, sterilization, and abortion. And they continue to insist on the right of married people, and not only Christians, to assistance from the State in making marriage and family life correspond to the will of God.

Graces of the Sacrament

In its longest single document, the Second Vatican Council went to great lengths to spell out the marvelous graces that Christ confers on His married followers.

Since the sacrament of Matrimony is to be a reflection of the selfless love of Christ for His Church, the principal grace of this sacrament is the gift of selfless love.

> Christ our Lord has abundantly blessed this love, which is rich in its various features, coming as it does from the spring of divine love and modeled on Christ's own union with the Church. Just as of old God encountered His people with a covenant of love and fidelity, so our Savior, the Spouse of the Church, now encounters Christian spouses through the sacrament of Marriage. He abides in them in order that by their mutual self-giving, spouses will love each other with enduring fidelity, as He loved the Church and delivered Himself for her. . . .
>
> Marriage and married love are, by nature, ordered to the procreation and education of children . . . true married love and the whole structure of family life which results from it is directed to disposing the spouses to cooperate valiantly with the love of the Creator and Savior, who through them will increase and enrich His family

from day to day (*The Church in the Modern World*, 50).

The Church has summarized the graces of the sacrament of Marriage in two terms: "procreative love" and "unitive love."

By the grace of unitive love, married spouses are given supernatural light and strength to remain united and grow in their mutual charity all the days of their lives. But they also receive the grace to share their very being with others, who are not yet conceived or born. Their love is, therefore, also procreative, going outside themselves to the children that God wants to send them. After the children are brought into the world, the sacrament further enables father and mother to provide for the bodily and spiritual needs of their offspring.

PART THREE

THE WILL
OF
GOD

CHRISTIAN MORALITY

In order to reach heaven, we must have the grace of God. Beyond what we have when we enter this world, we need divine grace in order to reach ever-lasting life in the world to come.

The main source of this grace is the sacraments, beginning with Baptism. And the most important of the sacraments to keep us spiritually alive and well is the Holy Eucharist.

But the sacraments alone are not enough. We must cooperate with the graces we receive. God keeps giving us constant illuminations of the mind and inspirations of the will, and we must respond to these divine visitations. We must be mentally alert to what God is telling us He wants. And we must be ready with our wills to choose what He tells us to do.

The English word "morality" is misleading. We speak of something a person does as "moral" or "im-moral," to describe something "good" or "bad." Properly speaking, however, every action we perform with conscious awareness of what we are doing, and freely choose to do it—is a moral action. There are therefore morally good and morally bad actions. If the action is done consciously and voluntarily, it is a moral action. And if what we choose to do is what God wants us to do, it is morally good. Otherwise it is morally bad.

If we further ask: Why does God want us to do certain things? The answer is because He knows that certain actions will lead us to heaven.

Our main task on earth is to decide with our minds and choose with our wills what God tells us will bring us to heaven. Nothing else really matters during the few years we have between birth and death. Our main purpose is to live a good moral life here, so we may enjoy a happy eternal life hereafter.

Basic Principles

We see immediately that the foundation of all morality is knowledge and freedom.

Knowledge means that we know in our minds what we should do to reach heaven. When what we think should be done is what God wants us to do, we have the truth. In other words, truth is the agreement of mind with reality. And reality in moral matters is what God knows and tells us will bring us to our final destiny.

Freedom means that our wills are not compelled to do something. They are not forced either by some pressure from outside of us, or compelled by some power inside of us, to do what our mind informs us is desirable. We are free because we can choose what we want. Of course, we are truly free when we are at liberty to choose to do what is morally good and choose not to do what is morally bad.

There is a close relationship between knowledge and freedom. Before we can choose anything we must first know what to choose. Our wills must be informed by our minds that something is desirable. The person, place, or thing must at least appear to be good before we can reasonably choose it.

Sources of Moral Knowledge. There are, in general, two sources of knowledge available to us to help us to live a good moral life: They are reason and revelation.

Our reason has the natural ability to learn what is the right course of action to follow in a given situation. By reflecting on ourselves and other people, we can obtain some knowledge of what is right and wrong, at least in some basic areas of human behavior.

Thus our reason can attain some knowledge of the existence of God as a Supreme Being whom we should obey, and to whom we should pray. Our reason, too, can conclude that because we want others to respect our life and property, we should act the same way toward them. Therefore hurting or killing another human being, or stealing from someone is wrong. We expect others, when they talk to us, to be honest in what they say. So we naturally conclude that when we speak to others, we should not tell a lie.

But our minds have been darkened by original sin, and further darkened by living in a sin-laden world, and even more darkened by our own personal sins. That is why God has seen fit to teach the human race, by His special revelation, many things that we might otherwise not all know, or know as well as we need to reach our heavenly home.

We may safely assume that God began this special revelation of His will at the dawn of human history. But once He called the children of Abraham to be His Chosen People, He revealed to them many duties that have since become the common possession of the human family. The single most important summary of these duties is the Ten Commandments.

When God became man in the person of Christ, He did not do away with the commandments of the Old Law. But He developed and deepened them beyond anything that was known before. That is why, when we speak of Christian morality, we mean all that Jesus Christ meant when He told the apostles to teach all nations to observe everything that He commanded. This "everything" includes whatever human reason can know about the divine will, whatever God revealed since the dawn of human history, and whatever Jesus taught we must do to return to the God from whom we came.

The Church's Role as Teacher of Morality. Christ did not leave His followers without a living guide. That is why He founded the Church. She was to keep intact the truths of faith which His followers were to believe. She was to remain the universal sacrament of salvation, as the channel of grace so that those who believe might live on in a blessed eternity. But she was also, and with emphasis, to continue teaching and explaining the moral responsibilities of historic Christianity.

A Catholic catechism has always contained these three essentials: the faith to be believed, the sacraments to be received, and the commandments to be observed. But in modern times, there is a special—and crucial—need for understanding how Christians are to live by their obedience to the will of God.

The key to this moral understanding is the teaching authority of the Church, vested in the successors of the apostles in union with the successor of St. Peter.

The Conscience

Given the foregoing principles, it is obvious what the Church understands by the conscience. Conscience is the practical judgment that a person makes whether a particular action is morally good or bad. Conscience is the mind deciding on the morality of a given action. But the basis of this decision is always our human reason enlightened by faith in God's revealed truth as taught by the Catholic Church.

Seen in this way, it becomes clear that we must always follow our conscience. But we have the prior responsibility of making sure that our conscience is properly educated. There are objective norms of morality, and it is our duty to learn these norms from prudent reflection on the world in which we live, from humble acceptance of divine revelation, and from sincere obedience to the Church's magisterium or teaching authority.

Virtues and Vices

Experience tells us that we develop moral habits according to our fidelity to the voice of conscience.

There is an iron law in the formation of habits. Apart from the supernatural action of divine grace, we can acquire good moral habits, called virtues, as we can acquire bad moral habits or vices. The law which underlines all formation of habit says that every thought tends to become a desire, every desire tends to become an action, and every action tends to become a habit.

Consequently, there is no such thing as a sterile thought. We conceive a thought and, unless checked, it grows into a desire. The same holds true of our desires. Unless checked, they become actions. And so, too, with actions. Simply because I have performed any action, interior or exterior, it spontaneously grows into a habit by sheer repetition.

Moral Virtues. Unlike the theological virtues of faith, hope, and charity, the moral virtues are immediately directed toward morally good actions.

1. Prudence enables us to make correct moral judgments. A prudent person can recognize what needs to be done, and what morally good means should be used to do what is pleasing to God. St.

Thomas Aquinas teaches that prudence is composed of no less than eight elements:

- the memory of past experiences on which a person draws when making a moral decision
- understanding of the basic principles of morality, derived from reason and revelation
- docility or the willingness to learn from others, especially those of mature age and experience
- shrewdness in being able to make a wise conjecture about the best course of action to follow in a particular case
- reason or the ability to apply general principles to a concrete situation
- foresight is the single most important part of prudence. The very word "prudence" means being able to provide or foresee how something should be done
- circumspection takes into account the circumstances under which we plan to do something. Thus the time, place, and persons involved have an important bearing on the morality of our actions
- caution is the final ingredient of prudence which anticipates the evils or harm that an otherwise good action may occasion or produce

2. Justice concerns our dealings with others. Unlike prudence, justice is a virtue of the will. It

respects the rights of others, that is, the rights of God and of our neighbor.

There is a profound sense in which we are to practice justice toward God. And we have come to call this justice the virtue of religion. Religion means respecting the rights of God as our Creator and Lord. Everything we are, and have and hope to become and possess, come from Him. He therefore has a right to our recognition and respect, to our gratitude, and love, to our obedience and submission to His will.

There are two forms of virtue in our dealings with others, namely commutative and distributive justice. While both concern our respecting the rights of other people, they differ in the relationships that we have with one another.

There is first of all the mutual relationship between people. As individuals, each of us has certain rights that another person is to respect. When I recognize the rights of another, I practice commutative or mutual justice. Each of us has a right to be treated as a person who has certain needs like food, shelter, and rest for the body; like attention and affection and acceptance for the soul. Each of us has a right to fulfill these needs and to possess the necessary means to their fulfillment. Others are to honor these rights and not deprive us of what we possess or need to acquire to live as human beings with an eternal destiny.

But we are also members of a natural society like the family or State, and the supernatural society of the Church. Those who hold authority have the duty to provide the members with all the means necessary to fulfill their respective role in the society to which they belong. Indeed they have a right to these necessary means. And when those in authority respect these rights, they are practicing distributive justice by distributing to those under their care each one's just and proportionate share.

3.   Fortitude is the virtue of the will which controls our natural fears. We are afraid of pain, whether bodily or spiritual, and instinctively draw away from a painful experience. But immediately we must distinguish two kinds of fear, which call for two different forms of fortitude.

The first kind of fear arises from the prospect of doing something difficult. It may be as simple a thing as writing a letter or as important as entering marriage, or as demanding as a vocation to the consecrated life. In this case, we need courage to do what conscience tells us we should, or even undertake a lifetime responsibility that is clearly God's will. Our wills are weakened by sin and therefore shrink from either starting or persevering in what our better judgment says should be undertaken or carried through.

The second kind of fear is different. What we dread is our own weakness in enduring trial or suffering that God sends us. It may be sickness or disability, rejection by someone we love, or opposition from persons who were formerly friends.

The pain may be in the body, the emotions, or in the depths of the soul. And we are all too aware of the strength it will take to suffer without complaining, not to say to remain calm and cheerful under duress.

Fortitude is necessary to cope with both kinds of fear. But the second kind of fortitude, faith tells us, is especially needed to remain loyal in following Christ. More than once, the Master predicted that to be His disciples we must resign ourselves to carry the Cross. That is why Christian fortitude is, above all, the courage of patience.

4. Temperance, like fortitude, is a virtue of the will that controls our natural impulses. But whereas fortitude protects us from running away from pain, temperance preserves us from running toward sinful pleasures. Temperance controls our spontaneous desires.

There would have been no need for temperance, as we now understand it, except that we have a fallen human nature. We are drawn to whatever pleases us, regardless of whether or not what we desire is morally good. We need food and drink, clothing and shelter, sleep and rest for the body. In order to survive, the human race needs to reproduce itself. On the mental level, we need to acquire knowledge; on the social level we need acceptance, companionship, and understanding love.

But our wants tend to exceed our needs, and

our needs do not always correspond to our wants. There is imbalance between reality and desire. This is where temperance is not only useful or important. It is absolutely necessary if we are to be at peace in this world, and attain the happiness, for which we were created, in the world to come. Temperance is at once a brake and an accelerator. As a brake, it keeps our desires from getting out of control; it tempers our urges to make sure they correspond to what reason and faith tell us is really, and not only apparently, good for us. As an accelerator, temperance stimulates our dormant impulses to want what we should desire, even when we have to rouse ourselves to seek what we need.

There is a close connection between fortitude and temperance. In order to control our desires and direct them toward what God wants us to do, we need courage, especially the courage to face difficulties and not collapse under the sometimes heavy demands of Providence. But fortitude also requires temperance, because we need motivation to sustain us under trial. Part of this motivation is the desire to obtain the reward, already in this life, that God has promised those who courageously submit to His divine will.

As with fortitude, so temperance has been immensely elevated by the coming of Christ. He has given His followers such powerful reasons for self-control as were never known before. He has also given us such good things to desire as were unknown in the annals of human history. By His grace He made available supernatural means to subdue our irrational drives. And by the same grace He has made it possible to aspire to become like Him who is our God.

Capital Sins.   Technically speaking, a vice is a bad moral habit. Just as the repetition of good moral actions gradually develops into the corresponding virtues, so the repetition of sinful acts induces sinful habits that we call vices.

However, there is more at work here than merely human psychology. No doubt, habits are produced by repeatedly performing certain acts. If I hold back my temper every time I am provoked to anger, I will acquire the virtue of patience. And if I regularly give in to my love of ease, I will acquire the habit of laziness.

But Christianity teaches that we have a fallen human nature. Since the fall of our first parents, even though we recover the supernatural life through Baptism, we have sinful tendencies that remain with us until death. There tendencies have come to be called "capital sins." We may say they are the main, or capital inclinations we have to commit sin.

Scriptures may even call them "sins." But the Church tells us they are not really sins. Rather they come from sin, and unless resisted they lead to sin.

1.   Pride, as a sinful inclination, is the inordinate desire for self-esteem. In relation to God, we were nothing until, in His almighty love, He brought us into existence, and except for His sustaining

hand, we would lapse into the nothingness from which we came.

The problem is that we tend to forget who God is and who we are. The most fundamental form of pride, therefore, is to think of oneself independently of God.

The further problem is that we not only tend to take other people for granted, and forget how much we owe to everyone whom God has put into our lives, but we are slow to recognize the good qualities of others, and become preoccupied with ourselves.

The remedy for pride is a sincere knowledge of self, especially of one's sinfulness. We must pray for humility and accept the humiliations permitted by divine Providence.

2. Lust is an inordinate desire for sexual pleasure. There is a God-given desire for sexual pleasure within the sanctity of marriage. But the urge is so strong that it requires the constant help of divine grace to be kept under control.

In order to master the sexual passion, it is necessary to control one's thoughts. But there can be no control of the mind without constant discipline of the senses, especially the eyes.

3. Avarice is the disorderly love of material possessions. Greed is extreme avarice. We need material things in order to serve God in this world of space and time. But the world is so attractive and its pleasures so seductive, that our fallen nature wants to acquire far beyond what we need. Ava-

rice is the desire to accumulate, which has become an addiction.

Avarice must be controlled by an interior detachment from worldly possessions. Daily reflection on the passing nature of everything in this life is necessary to free one's heart from sinful attachment to material things.

4. Envy is the sadness felt when another person has something which is considered detrimental to one's own reputation or self-esteem. Envy is a deeply interior urge that demands careful watchfulness. The surest remedy, with God's help, is the practice of selfless charity.

5. Anger, as a sinful tendency, is the inordinate desire to remove obstacles or difficulties that stand in our way. Anger can be sinless, and even virtuous, as when Moses was angry with the rebellious Israelites, and Jesus was angry with the money-changers in the temple.

What makes anger sinful is either the cause of the anger or its intensity or duration. It is righteous indignation when there is a justified reason for becoming angry, and the intensity or duration is kept under reasonable control.

The surest way to control one's temper is to develop the habit of patient thoughts. Keeping one's mind off things which annoy or irritate us is necessary if we are to acquire the habit of patience.

6. Gluttony is an unreasonable desire for food or drink. As with the other capital sins, it is not

the desire that is wrong, but that it gets out of control.

Mortification of one's appetite is a proven way of mastering the urge to gluttony. This means not only controlling the amount of food and drink to reasonable limits, but also avoiding self-indulgence in taste and extravagance. There is such a thing as luxury in food and drink that a follower of Christ should mortify. Moreover, abstinence may be necessary, especially in the use of alcohol or other addictive satisfaction of the palate.

7. Sloth is the desire for ease, even at the expense of doing the known will of God. Whatever we do in life requires effort. Everything we do is to be a means of salvation. The slothful person is unwilling to do what God wants because of the effort it takes to do it. There is such a thing as weariness in well-doing. Sloth becomes a sin when it slows down and even brings to a halt the energy we must expend in using the means to salvation. Sloth is mainly psychological.

Sloth and laziness are not the same thing as fatigue. We need a break and relaxation from work. But we give in to sloth when we are unwilling to pay the price of exertion in doing what reason and faith tell us God wants us to do.

Remedies for sloth are frequent reflections on the harm it causes, by developing the habits of punctuality, prudent planning, and meditation on divine justice in rewarding human effort and punishing laziness in the service of God.

THE TEN COMMANDMENTS

The Ten Commandments are also called the Decalogue, from the Greek *deka*, ten, and *logos*, word. They are therefore the Ten Words of God which synthesize God's covenant with His chosen people.

They were divinely revealed to Moses on Mount Sinai and engraved on two tablets of stone. Moses broke the stone tablets in anger when he came down from the mountain and saw the people practicing idolatry. However, the tablets were later replaced and placed in the Ark of the Covenant.

There are two versions of the Ten Commandments, in Exodus 20:1–17 and Deuteronomy 5:6–18. Although very similar, they differ in various ways. In Exodus, for example, the observance of the Sabbath is based on a religious motive, namely weekly to commemorate Yahweh's resting on the seventh day after creating the world. In Deuteronomy, the Sabbath is a day of rest from labor, where the motive is more humanitarian. The two versions also differ on the prohibition of covetousness. In Exodus, a man's wife is classified along with his other possessions that others may not covet. In Deuteronomy, the wife is classified separately.

Christ did not suppress the Ten Commandments. He not only kept them as found in His Sermon on the Mount, but He deepened and elevated them far beyond what had been prescribed in the Old Law.

From the earliest days of the Church, the Ten Commandments held a central place in Christian instruction. According to St. Thomas Aquinas and St. Bonaventure, the Ten Commandments are really the Natural Law. The precepts of the Decalogue can be known by the light of reason without revelation. But God revealed them through Moses to the human race in order that everyone would know what the Creator requires of His creatures as a condition for attaining eternal life.

There is some difference in the numbering of the Ten Commandments. In the Greek, Anglican, and Protestant churches—excluding the Lutheran—the prohibition of false worship becomes two commandments; there is a separate commandment about "graven images." Then in order to keep the number ten, the precept against covetousness is combined with the prohibition of lustful desires.

In the Catholic Church, there is only one commandment against false worship. But there are two separate precepts against internal sins of lust and greed, as the ninth and tenth commandments. They correspond to the sixth and seventh precepts which forbid adultery and stealing.

In our treatment of the Ten Commandments, we shall consider each precept in two stages. First we will see *what* the commandment prescribes, not only in the Old Testament but also in our day. Then we will look more closely to find out *how* Christ elevated each precept and has guided His Church to teach the obligations of Christianity.

There is great practical value in examining the Decalogue in this way. For centuries now, the Church has had to insist on three doctrines that form the bedrock of Christian morality. They were defined in the sixteenth century.

1. The gospel commands more than merely faith, as though everything else is indifferent, and neither prescribed nor prohibited. The Ten Commandments are binding on all Christians.

2. A justified person, no matter how perfect he may be, is still bound to observe the Commandments of God and of the Church. It is not enough for him to simply believe. He must also observe the commandments because he does not have an unconditional and absolute promise of eternal life.

3. God has given Jesus Christ not only as a Redeemer in whom we are to trust, but also as a Lawgiver whom we are to obey (Council of Trent, January 13, 1547).

To be emphasized is that Christ is the Living God who became man to save us by teaching what we must do to reach heaven, and by providing the necessary grace "to observe all the commandments I gave you" (Matthew 28:20).

First Commandment

The wording of the First Commandment is exactly
the same in Exodus and in Deuteronomy.

> I am Yahweh, your God, who brought you out
> of the land of Egypt, out of the house of slavery.
> You shall have no gods except me (Exodus
> 20:1–3; Deuteronomy 5:6–7).

There follow after this statement of the First
Commandment, several verses of prohibition against
carved images. The Latin Rite of the Catholic
Church considers these verses an explanation of the
first precept.

> You shall not make yourself a carved image or
> any likeness of anything in heaven or on earth
> beneath or in the waters under the earth; you
> shall not bow down to them or serve them. For I,
> Yahweh, your God, am a jealous God and I pun-
> ish the father's faults in the sons, the grandsons
> and the great-grandsons of those who hate me;

but I show kindness to thousands of those who love me and keep my commandments (Exodus 20:4–6).

Centuries of Catholic commentary find two levels of meaning in the First Commandment: the expressed and the implied, and on both levels there is a positive declaration or command, and a negative prohibition.

Yahweh a Jealous God

God identifies Himself as Yahweh, which is also rendered as "Lord" or "Adonai." In the pre-Christian Greek translation, the title was understood to mean "He who is" and the Latin Vulgate explains it to mean "I am who am." By implication, therefore, Yahweh is the Being who simply *is*. He never came into existence because He always was. By further implication, He is the One who brings all other beings into existence because He is their Creator.

The word "jealous," when applied to God, means that He wants to be recognized for who He is, and does not want any creature to be given the honors which are due to the Creator.

That is why God forbids anyone or anything to be worshipped as though it were divine. The Bible makes constant reference to the gods of the Gentiles. And pre-Christian history shows how widespread was polytheism or the worship of many gods and goddesses.

The basic issue was not so much a question of numbers, but rather that there is only one God. The focus of the First Commandment is that there is only one Necessary Being, who cannot not exist. Everything else in the universe exists only because He brought it and keeps it in existence.

The worship of any creature by paying it divine homage is a lie. There are no other gods. There is only one God. He demands to be recognized for who He is: the One Being from whom all other beings receive their existence, and by whom they are constantly sustained.

It is only logical that He will punish those who refuse to honor Him as their God, and shows kindness to those who love Him by keeping His commandments.

The prohibition of carved images should be seen against this background. What is really forbidden is not carved images as such. It is the worship of creatures, which can be represented in images, instead of worshipping the invisible God, who cannot be depicted in pictures or carved in wood or stone.

Adoration, Prayer and Sacrifice

Underlying the First Commandment is the duty to practice the virtue of religion. This is the moral virtue which disposes us to give God the worship He deserves. He is our Creator and Lord; therefore, we owe Him submission. He is our Destiny; therefore, we owe Him our love.

Adoration. Only God deserves to be adored, because only God is the First Cause of the universe from whom everything came and on whose almighty power everything depends. As our Creator, we owe Him the adoration of obedience to His laws.

But God is also to be adored because He is the One for whom we were made. He wants to give us Himself, finally, in eternal happiness in heaven. We should, therefore, adore Him also with our selfless love, desiring to be united with Him, even as He wants to be united with us.

If the adoration of obedience means total submission to the almighty will of God, the adoration of love means total generosity in giving ourselves beyond the demands of justice, to the One who loves us with an everlasting love.

The principal way that we adore God is by prayer and sacrifice.

Prayer. The voluntary response to the awareness of God's presence is prayer. When we pray, we are doing what God mainly wants us to do in life: He wants us to communicate with Him. When we pray we are doing several things:

- We become mentally aware of God's presence.

- We respond to this awareness by raising our minds and hearts to God.

• We talk to God, sharing our thoughts and desires with Him.

Our prayerful conversation with God may take on any one of several forms. We may adore God by telling Him we recognize that He is Lord and we are the creatures of His hands. We may adore God by telling Him we love Him with our whole heart. We may thank God for all the blessings He has bestowed on us and on others. We may beg for His mercy for the sins we and others have committed against Him. And we may ask Him for the graces that we and others need to reach the heavenly beatitude for which we were made.

Implied in every form of prayer is the adoration of obedience and love.

Sacrifice. The highest form of prayer is sacrifice. This is the willing surrender of something precious to God. As with adoration, there are two basic forms of sacrifice. There is the sacrifice of submission. Here we give up some creature that we like in order to express our total dependence on God's will. There is also the sacrifice of love. Here we surrender something pleasant in order to please the God whom we love.

Sacrifice presumes there are precious things in life: our bodily strength and life, material possessions and acceptance by others, emotional health and physical comfort, friends and the company of congenial persons. All of these, in different ways, God either will or may take away. And we are as pleasing to Him as we are willing to give them up, according to His mysterious will.

The soul of sacrifice is internal surrender. We not only let go of some creature that God is removing—or wants us to remove—but we let go with our hearts. We surrender our free wills freely to the will of God. Why? Because then we show that we really love Him, not only in words which are easy, but in action, which is hard. And the hardest action we can perform is to let go of our self-will.

The most perfect sacrifice we can offer is the Sacrifice of the Mass, in which we join our self-surrender with that of Christ, who offers Himself and us to the heavenly Father.

Moreover, since we believe that God became man, we are to adore Jesus Christ, who is true God. We are to pray to Him as our God. We are to sacrifice ourselves *for* Him, because He is God, and *like* Him, because He became man to show us how the human will should surrender itself to the God of love.

Sins of Irreligion

There is a correct sense in which the First Commandment contains the nine other commandments that follow. Anyone who is sincerely trying to live out the First Commandment is living out the whole Decalogue.

For this reason, we can say that sins against the First Commandment are beyond counting. Every sin is an offense against God, who has a right to our obedience and a claim to our love. Consequently, every sin, at root, is an offense against the First Commandment.

However, there are certain sins that the history of Christian morality has come to associate as more directly against the First Commandment. They are idolatry and superstition, tempting God, sacrilege, and simony. A general name for these is irreligion which is contrary to the primary virtue prescribed by the First Commandment, namely, the virtue of religion.

Idolatry. The word "idolatry" means the worship of idols. It is the sin of giving divine honors to a creature. In the early Church, the followers of Christ were put to death for refusing to worship idols, even externally. Modern secularism is idolatry in practice. Money and pleasure, sex and power, science and the media can all be idolized. The key to protecting oneself from practical idolatry is always to use creatures according to the will of God. They are to be means of reaching Him and never an end in themselves.

Satanism is a form of idolatry. Widely practiced under various names among polytheists who worship evil deities, it has become prevalent in western countries. Modern Satanism believes in two creator gods, one good and the other evil. Satanists venerate what Christians call Lucifer.

Superstition. Although various practices are called superstitions, strictly speaking superstition is unseemly or unbecoming worship of God.

This unbecoming worship may be the result of false devotion or of a tendency to magic. As false devotion, superstition has one feature in common. A person is concerned that unless certain external practices are performed, like multiplication of prayers, God will be displeased. When superstition tends toward magic, it associates God's blessings with the veneration of unapproved objects or belief in unverified revelations or the performance of unauthorized ritual.

Tempting God. This is the sin of doing or omitting something in order to test one of God's attributes, especially His love, wisdom, or power.

An explicit tempting of God is done when a person deliberately puts God to the test. Such would be telling God to work a miracle as a person throws himself over a cliff; or an atheist boasting that if there is a God, "let Him strike me dead." These are grave crimes.

But implicit tempting of God is more common. Thus it is tempting God to expect Him to provide the grace we need to fulfill our duties in life without prayer.

Sacrilege. Violation of a sacred person, place, or object is sacrilege. Also called desecration, it is a grave sin that has been many times condemned in the Bible, especially in the Second Book of Maccabees and the letters of St. Paul.

Implied in the sin of sacrilege is the divine precept of treating whatever belongs to God as something holy. Desecration is, therefore, an insult to God. St. Paul condemns sacrilegious reception of Holy Communion (I Corinthians 11:27–29).

Simony. Named after Simon Magus (Acts 8:18) who tried to buy spiritual powers from St. Peter, simony is the sacrilege of buying or selling what is spiritual in return for money. It is forbidden by the divine law. Thus to promise prayers in exchange for money is simony. To give or obtain ecclesiastical authority in exchange for some material grant is simony.

The Church recognizes the right to receive an offering for some spiritual service, as a personal gift to the one who performs the service. Mass stipends are permissible, but carefully regulated by Church law.

SECOND COMMANDMENT

In both Exodus and Deuteronomy, the wording of the Second Commandment is the same.

> You shall not utter the name of Yahweh, your God, to misuse it, for Yahweh will not leave unpunished the man who utters His name to misuse it (Exodus 20:7; Deuteronomy 5:11).

The Second Commandment is really an expression of the preceding. It prescribes the respectful use of God's name and forbids using the Divine Name irreverently. Implied in this precept is the duty to profess by verbal communication our belief in the one true God.

Vocal Prayer

From the earliest days of the Chosen People, vocal prayers were part of Israel's religious history. Prayer in the Old Testament is addressed to God alone, both because only God deserves to be praised as man's Creator and because in Him alone is our salvation.

Because of the social character of ancient Israel, vocal prayers and hymns in common were of primary importance. The books of the Old Testament are filled with such forms of communication with Yahweh. The Psalms alone are one hundred and fifty religious lyrics that have also become part of the Christian liturgy.

As we enter the New Testament, we find Christ urging His followers to pray, not only privately but together. At the same time, He was very critical of some practices of prayer among the Pharisees. He denounced their hypocrisy, describing them as "devouring the houses of widows while they make long prayers in public (Mark 12:40; Luke 20:47). When Jesus was asked by His disciples to teach them how to pray, He gave them the Our Father.

Following the custom of the Israelites, the early Christians sang ritual hymns in their public assemblies (Acts 16:25). In this they were putting into practice what St. Paul told the Ephesians:

Sing the words and tunes of the psalms and hymns when you are together, and go on singing and chanting to the Lord in your hearts, so that always and everywhere you are giving thanks to God who is our Father, in the name of our Lord Jesus Christ (Ephesians 5:19).

While encouraging vocal prayers, the Church wants us to be aware of what we are saying or singing. It is one thing to pronounce the words; it is something else to unite oneself in mind and heart with God whom we are addressing. There is such a thing as culpable inattention in vocal prayer, and therefore a sin against the Second Commandment.

Oaths and Vows

An oath is the invocation of God's name to bear witness to the truth of what someone is saying. The oath may be either assertive or promissory. It is assertive when the Divine Name is called upon in testimony of the truth of some past or present fact or event, for example, that a crime was not committed. The oath is promissory when a person calls upon God to testify that a promise made will be kept.

In the Old Testament, oaths were to be made by Yahweh alone. They were, in effect, a profession of faith in the divinity of the one invoked. Therefore, to swear by other gods was a denial of the exclusive divinity of the one true God.

At the same time, an oath is such a serious use of God's name, that it may not be taken lightly. The norms for a proper oath were set down by Jeremiah when he said, "If you swear, 'As Yahweh lives!' truthfully, justly, honestly, the nations will bless themselves by you" (Jeremiah 4:2). An oath must be in witness of the truth; otherwise it becomes perjury. It must be taken prudently; otherwise it becomes a desecration of God's majesty. It must be expressed honestly, which means that an oath may not be taken to witness to something sinful.

A vow differs from a promissory oath in promising God to do something which is better than its opposite or omission. Vows are often mentioned in the Old Testament and go back to the earliest history of Israel. Jacob made a vow to worship at Bethel (Genesis 28:20); Hannah made a vow in order to obtain a son (I Samuel 1:11); David vowed to provide a dwelling for the Ark (Psalm 132:2). There are frequent references in the Old Law to the duty of keeping a vow (Psalm 22:26, 50:14; Job 22:27; Isaiah 19:21).

In the New Testament, there are two explicit references to vows (Acts 18:18, 21:23–24). But we know from tradition that Christians took vows already in the apostolic age.

According to the Church's teaching, a vow is a free and deliberate promise made to God to do something that is morally good and more pleasing to God than its omission. Always understood is that a person would commit a sin by violating the promise. Vows are pleasing to God because in taking them a person goes beyond the call of duty to be generous with God.

The most familiar vows in the Catholic Church are those taken to practice the evangelical counsels of consecrated chastity, poverty, and obedience. They are called counsels to distinguish them from evangelical precepts, which are binding on all the faithful under sin.

In the vow of chastity, a person promises God to sacrifice marriage. In vowing poverty, the promise is to give up material possessions. And in the vow of obedience, a person agrees before God to submit to the authority of someone in an institute of consecrated life.

Vows are praiseworthy because they unite the one taking the vow by a new bond with God. Actions performed under vow become also acts of religion. Vows give to God not only a single morally good action; they dedicate a person's will to the Almighty. Vows also forestall human weakness by meriting special grace from God to perform actions that might otherwise be humanly impossible.

Blasphemy and Cursing

Sins against the Second Commandment include every failure in vocal prayer, and every offense against God in taking an oath or making a vow. But there are two sins against this commandment that deserve special attention. They are blasphemy and cursing.

Blasphemy is every form of speaking against God in a scornful or abusive way. Blasphemy need not be expressed in speech. It can be purely internal in thought or desire. And it can become externally manifest in actions that are blasphemous twice over: once because of the internal contempt for God which inspires the action, and once again because the blasphemer goes so far as to profess his opposition to God so that others are scandalized by the blasphemy.

Since Jesus Christ is true God, any thought or desire, word or action that is scornful of Him is blasphemous.

There is, of course, a difference between conscious and deliberate blasphemy and blasphemy that arises from emotion or ignorance. Depending on a person's responsibility for his ignorance or emotional condition, the guilt of blasphemy must be judged accordingly. One thing, however, is certain. Our knowledge of God is a duty, and control of our emotions is an obligation of the moral law. We should know who God is, that He deserves our total reverence of His name, and we have a free will that, with God's grace, is to master our feelings. Most cases of blasphemy arise under pressure of the emotions, especially resentment against God because of the suffering that human beings have to endure. The secret is to develop such a strong faith that even the hardest trials of life will be seen as visitations of a loving God.

Cursing is the sin of calling on God to inflict some evil or injury on someone. In a way, cursing is a form of blasphemy. Every curse arises from hatred of another person, to the point of wanting that person to suffer at the hands of God.

The malice of cursing is twofold. It is a grave sin against charity. To love someone is to wish well for that person. To curse someone is to wish evil for that person. But cursing is also sinful because it invokes the name of a loving God to ask that someone be harmed. Cursing, therefore, is not only a failure in love. It is hatred put into practice, and asks God to confirm this hatred by injuring the one who is hated.

The devil hates human beings because he envies their prospect of heaven. Those who curse others are imitating the evil spirit.

THIRD COMMANDMENT

The longest biblical text in the Decalogue is for the Third Commandment.

While both Exodus and Deuteronomy prescribe the Sabbath, the motive and the manner of its observance are different. Both passages, though lengthy, should be quoted in full.

In Exodus, the Sabbath is a weekly commemoration of God's creation.

> Remember the sabbath day and keep it holy. For six days you shall labor and do your work, but the seventh is a sabbath for Yahweh, your God. You shall do no work that day, neither you nor your son nor your daughter nor your servants, men or women, nor your animals, nor the stranger who lives with you. For in six days Yahweh made the heavens and the earth and the sea and all that these hold, but on the seventh day He rested; that is why Yahweh has blessed the sabbath day and made it sacred (Exodus 20:8–11).

In Deuteronomy, the Sabbath is prescribed as a weekly commemoration of God's deliverance of His people, as the following words indicate:

> Observe the sabbath day and keep it holy, as Yahweh, your God, has commanded you . . . Remember that you were a servant in the land of Egypt, and that Yahweh, your God, brought you out from there with mighty hand and outstretched arm; because of this, Yahweh, your God, has commanded you to keep the sabbath day (Deuteronomy 5:12–15).

No Jewish observance figures more prominently in the New Testament than the Sabbath. Christianity retained the Sabbath and elevated it to a unique dignity.

Old Testament Observance

Observing the Sabbath was one of the most important precepts of pre-Christian Judaism. It was developed independent of the temple and became identified with the synagogue, even among the Jews of the dispersion, who lived far from Jerusalem. The Sabbath marked off the Jewish people from the Gentiles, and for much of their history was the one visible sign of being a true Israelite.

As the rabbis began to explain the meaning of the Sabbath rest, a variety of interpretations arose. There were no less than thirty-nine types of work classified by experts in Judaic law. Forbidden on the Sabbath were the lighting of fire, clapping the hands, visiting the sick, and walking beyond a certain distance. A Sabbath day's journey, referred to by St. Luke, was about three thousand feet (Acts 1:12), unless a person set up a temporary domicile by depositing a personal possession some distance from home.

New Testament Teaching

Jesus observed the Sabbath according to reasonable standards, and occasionally taught in the synagogues on the Sabbath (Mark 6:2; Luke 4:16, 31).

But soon the Pharisees began to criticize His disciples for rubbing grain between their hands on the Sabbath, which was condemned as work. Christ was especially severe in rebuking those who condemned His performing miracles of healing on the Sabbath.

His decisive teaching is summed up in the sentence that, "The Sabbath was made for man, not man for the Sabbath; so the Son of Man is master even of the Sabbath" (Mark 2:27). In saying this, Jesus laid the foundation for the Christian observance of the Third Commandment. There is, indeed, to be one day set aside each week to become what it now is, the Lord's Day. But the emphasis is to be on giving the day to the Lord.

There are references in apostolic times to the reading of the prophets and the Pentateuch (first five books of the Bible) on the Sabbath to present the gospel to Jewish audiences (Acts 13:14, 16:13). But soon the Judaizing Christians tried to impose the Sabbath observance on Gentile Christians. The result was that Paul declared that no one may be held bound to observe the Sabbath (Colossians 2:16), until finally Christians were completely freed from the Jewish obligations of the Sabbath law.

Sunday Observance

The name "Sunday" for the first day of the week was borrowed from the Romans who had borrowed it from the Egyptians. It was dedicated among the pagans to the sun which was worshipped as a god. But already in the first century, Christians understood Christ as the "Sun of Justice" (Malachi 4:2), and therefore the one true God who became man. He was the one whom they worshipped on Sunday.

Moreover, the name in Christian language was changed to the "Lord's Day," as used by St. John the Apostle during his exile for the faith. "I was on the island of Patmos," he wrote, "for having preached God's word and witnessed for Jesus; it was the Lord's Day and the Spirit possessed me" (Revelation 1:10).

The Christian practice of meeting on the first day of the week to celebrate the Eucharistic Sacrifice is clearly described in the Acts of the Apostles and in St. Paul (Acts 20:7; I Corinthians 16:2). In *The Teaching of the Twelve Apostles* (first century), the faithful are told, "On the Lord's Day, assemble in common to break bread and offer thanks *(euchariste-*

sate); but first confess your sins, so that your sacrifice may be pure: *(Didache* 14).

St. Ignatius of Antioch (died 107 A.D.) speaks of Christians as "no longer observing the Sabbath but living in the observance of the Lord's Day, on which also our Lord rose again" *(Letter to the Magnesians,* 9).

With the end of the great persecutions in the early fourth century, the Church began to make laws on the proper observance of Sunday. Thus in Spain, the bishops legislated that, "If anyone in the city neglects to come to church for three Sundays, let him be excommunicated for a short time so that he may be corrected" (Council of Elvira, 306 A.D.). About the same time laws were passed requiring the faithful to hear Mass and rest from servile work on Sunday. In drafting these laws, it was stated that both practices go back to the teaching of the apostles.

Over the centuries, Sunday became established as the principal feast day, each week, for the faithful. Three reasons were given:

1) It is the first day, the day on which God, changing darkness and matter, created the world (St. Justin Martyr, 165 A.D.).

2) It is the day on which Jesus Christ our Savior rose from the dead (St. Justin).

3) It is the day on which the Holy Spirit descended on Pentecost, in the form of tongues of fire (St. Isidore of Seville, 636 A.D.).

Church's Legislation

The new Code of Canon Law opens its legislation on "Feast Days" with several canons pertaining to the proper observance of Sunday. It also identifies what have come to be called holy days of obligation.

> The Lord's Day, on which the Paschal Mystery is celebrated, is by apostolic tradition to be observed in the universal Church as the primary holy day of obligation. . . .
>
> In the same way the following holy days are to be observed: the Nativity of our Lord Jesus Christ, the Epiphany, the Ascension, the feast of the Body and Blood of Christ, the feast of Mary the Mother of God, her Immaculate Conception, her Assumption, the feast of St. Joseph, the feast of the Apostles, Saints Peter and Paul, and the feast of All Saints. . . .
>
> However, the Episcopal Conference may, with the prior approval of the Apostolic See, suppress certain holy days of obligation, or transfer them to a Sunday. . . .
>
> On Sundays and other holy days of obligation, the faithful are obliged to assist at Mass. They are also to abstain from such work or business that would inhibit the worship to be given to God, the joy proper to the Lord's Day, or the due relaxation of mind and body. . . .
>
> The obligation of assisting at Mass is satisfied

whenever Mass is celebrated in a Catholic rite, either on a holy day itself or on the evening of the previous day (Canons 1246–1248).

Accordingly, the Catholic Church's understanding of the Third Commandment could not be clearer. The faithful are gravely bound to worship together on Sundays and holy days of obligation by participating in the Sacrifice of the Mass. This is their primary obligation in observing this commandment of the Decalogue.

They are also to avoid such work or business as would either interfere with their worship of God, or prevent them from celebrating the Lord's Day with peaceful joy, or deprive them of such rest and relaxation of mind and body as every person requires.

Modern popes have been outspoken to public officials and heads of business and industry, urging them to give the people freedom to worship and rest on Sundays. Pope John XXIII called it "a heavy responsibility."

FOURTH COMMANDMENT

The first three commandments pertain to our relationship with God. They oblige us to recognize God as our Lord and Master, to honor His Name in language and song, and to pay Him public homage as a people whom He has called to be His own.

With the Fourth Commandment, we enter on a new relationship with God. If the first three commandments summarize what may be called "religion," the last seven synthesize "morality." From the fourth through the tenth precepts, our duties toward others are identified as the practical living out of our duties toward God.

The text of the fourth Commandment is almost the same in Exodus and Deuteronomy. But the latter contains the former and is more specific.

> Honor your father and your mother, as Yahweh, your God, has commanded you, so that you may have long life and may prosper in the land that Yahweh, your God, gives to you (Deuteronomy 5:16).

247

As given to Moses, the Fourth Commandment only directly obliges children to honor their parents. But already in the Old Testament and on through the New, it was understood to include respect and obedience to all legitimate authority.

There is a unique fitness, however, in stressing the honor that children owe their parents. If they are faithful as children in their respectful obedience to father and mother, they will have laid the foundation for a lifetime honor of all rightful authority.

Old Testament Teaching

The biblical precept tells children they must honor their father and mother. The basis for this duty is the commandment of God. And the twofold reward is a long life, blessed by God in the land promised the Chosen People by the Lord.

To honor one's parents means to respect them, no matter what their age or physical condition; to obey them in whatever they command in accordance with the will of God; and to assist them, especially in sickness, poverty, or their declining years.

Underlying this obligation is the virtue of piety, or devotion to the authors of one's being. Thus filial piety is an earthly expression of the heavenly duty to honor God, who is the primary Author of all created beings.

Elsewhere in the Old Testament, the corresponding duty of parents to their children is also revealed. If children are to honor their parents, parents are to nourish and provide for their children, teach them, and train them in the law of the Lord.

Only in this way can family life be developed. In the Old Testament, the family is seen as a religious unit. The Passover was celebrated each year within the family. Family solidarity was the bedrock of Israel as God's chosen ones. The individual depended on the family for protection and support. The family shared in the rewards and even the guilt of each of its members.

New Testament Revelation

The Fourth Commandment was immensely developed by the coming of Christ. He was conceived and born in a family, and he established the Church as the supernatural family of the New Covenant. And He clearly separated the Church from the State, while recognizing the rights of civil authority in temporal matters for the members of His kingdom on earth.

The Christian Family. When the Son of God became man, He came as a little child. After the finding in the temple, the evangelist simply says that Jesus went down with Mary and Joseph and "came to Nazareth, and was subject to them" (Luke 2:51).

In this, Christ became the model for the honor and obedience that children owe their parents. He had a human will which He freely subjected to the directions of His mother and foster father. Masters of the spiritual life have written extensively on the lesson that Christ teaches all of us—not only children—by His humble obedience at Nazareth. "Who is it that obeys," asks St. Bernard, "and to whom is he obedient? It is God that obeys man; God, I say, to whom the angels are subject, to whom the Principalities and Powers are obedient. God obeyed Mary, and not only Mary, but also Joseph because of her" (Sermon on "He was sent," 1).

In the Holy Family, Mary and Joseph became the pattern for parents to follow in the exercise of authority. Pope John Paul II makes a great deal of this:

> In the family, which is a community of persons, special attention must be devoted to the children by developing a profound respect for their personal dignity, and a great respect and generous concern for their rights. This is true for every child, but it becomes all the more urgent the smaller the child is and the more it is in need of everything, when it is sick, suffering, or handicapped (*Familiaris Consortio*, 26).

There is a closer relationship than is commonly thought between respect for the child by the parents and the child's respect for its parents. Obedience is owed to the parents, but there is such a thing as earning the respect of their children. The parents' esteem for their children's personal dignity is necessary if the children are to have a corresponding esteem for their parents.

Implied in respect and esteem is the underlying love that children should have for their parents.

Here, too, Christ is the model for children to imitate, seen in the deep love He had for Mary and Joseph.

Spiritual Childhood. Totally surpassing anything in the Old Testament is Christ's profound teaching on children. Children are to be loved. Taking a child, on one occasion, Jesus placed it in the midst of His disciples. After He embraced the child, He said to them: "Whosoever shall receive one such child as this in my name, receives me, And whoever receives me, receives not me but Him who sent me" (Mark 9:35–36).

When, on another occasion, the disciples rebuked the mothers who brought their children to Jesus so He might touch them, He, in turn, rebuked the disciples. "When Jesus saw this," we are told, "He was indignant and said to them, 'Let the little children come to me; do not stop them; for it is to such as these that the kingdom of God belongs.'" Then He set down the condition for salvation. "I tell you solemnly," Christ declared, "anyone who does not welcome the kingdom of God like a little child will never enter it" (Mark 10:13–15).

Only those will be saved who, during their lives on earth, have practiced the humility and obedience, the docility and simplicity that human history associates with children.

Thus, the same St. Paul who told children "be obedient to your parents in the Lord" (Ephesians 6:1), also told Christian believers to become "perfect children of God" (Philippians 2:15). If children have their duty toward parents, all followers of Christ have

251

their duty toward God. They are to be like children in their complete reliance on the One without whose love and omnipotence they would not even exist.

Obedience to Church Authority.   Christ repeatedly stressed the duty of obedience to the authority of the Church He was establishing. In His closing discourse to the disciples, He told them to teach all nations to observe all that He had commanded. This commission summarized the whole of the Savior's public ministry. He determined as certain that, when He left the earth in visible form, He would leave the apostles and their successors with the right to command others in His name.

Everything that we associate with the Fourth Commandment about children honoring and obeying their parents, can be applied, in principle, to the honor and obedience that the faithful owe to those who hold legitimate authority in the Catholic Church. Yet, as in the case of parents and children, this is a mutual responsibility of the faithful toward those in ecclesiastical authority and of those in authority toward the faithful.

The Church's law is unqualified about the duty of the faithful.

> Christ's faithful, conscious of their own responsibility, are bound to show Christian obedience to what the sacred pastors, who represent Christ, declare as teachers of the faith and prescribe as rulers of the Church (Canon 212).

At the same time, those holding authority to teach and govern the faithful also have their duties. There are at least a dozen provisions in Canon Law for bishops alone, legislating how they are to provide for the doctrinal, moral, and liturgical needs of the people under their care. This means that, "Christ's faithful have the right to be assisted by their pastors from the spiritual riches of the Church, especially by the word of God and the sacraments" (Canon 213).

Obedience to Civil Authority. From birth to His death, Christ practiced obedience to those in civil authority. His birth at Bethlehem was occasioned by a decree of the emperor, ordering a census of all the people in the Roman Empire. Christ's death in Jerusalem was ordered by the Roman procurator, who unjustly condemned Jesus to be crucified.

On one historic occasion, He carefully distinguished between the rights of the State and the rights of God. The chief priests and scribes sent agents to Jesus to find some grounds "to hand Him over to the jurisdiction of the governor." They hoped to trap Him into denying the authority of the State.

They put to Him this question, "Master, we know that you say and teach what is right; you favor no one, but teach the way of God in all honesty. Is it permissible for us to pay taxes to Caesar or not?" But He was aware of their cunning and said, "Show me a denarius. Whose head and name are on it?" "Caesar's," they said. "Well then," He said to them, "give back to Caesar what belongs to Caesar—and to God what belongs to God" (Luke 20:21–25).

Christ's reply has become the foundation of the Catholic Church's teaching on State authority. The State has authority from God to govern its citizens in what concerns the temporal affairs of this life. Citizens, therefore, have the duty to obey civil authority. But their obedience is conditional. The rights of God are not only primary: They are normative. Laws of the State and decrees of civil authority are binding in conscience only where and in so far as they conform to the laws of God.

"God wants you to be good citizens," St. Peter told the early Christians (I Peter 2:15). And St. Paul declared, "You must all obey the governing authorities" (Romans 13:1). Yet Peter and Paul finally laid down their lives for Christ because their teaching was in conflict with the paganism of the State.

Civil authority is to be obeyed. But one of the gravest trials of Christ's followers in the modern world is the widespread denial of their religious rights by the secular State. "There are forms of government," the Second Vatican Council declared, "under which the public authorities strive to deter the citizens from professing their religion and make life particularly difficult and dangerous for religious bodies" (*Declaration on Religious Liberty*, 15).

The norm to be followed has not changed over the centuries. What Peter and the apostles told the Sanhedrin is just as true today: "Obedience to God comes before obedience to men" (Acts 5:29). The price for this statement has been martyrdom.

FIFTH COMMANDMENT

The wording of the Fifth Commandment is identical in the two biblical texts of the Decalogue, "You shall not kill" (Exodus 20:13; Deuteronomy 20:5–17).

Already in the Old Testament the prohibition was understood to mean "You shall not murder." Always understood was that it was forbidden to kill an innocent person.

The first recorded crime in the moral degradation after the Fall was the murder of Abel by his envious brother Cain (Genesis 4:1–16). Cain's punishment by God reveals the gravity of the sin of murder. Several times, the prophets mention murder among the crimes for which Israel would be punished by Yahweh (Isaiah 1:21; Jeremiah 7:9).

Yet, as we read the history of the Old Covenant, we are struck by the moral development introduced into the world by the coming of Christ. We are told, for example, that "If a man beats his slave, male or female, and the slave dies at his hands, he must pay the penalty. But should the slave survive for one or two days, he shall pay no penalty because the slave is his by right of purchase" (Exodus 21:20–21).

The Sermon on the Mount reveals how deeply Christ's teaching elevated the tenor of the Fifth Commandment. Jesus repeated the prohibition of the Decalogue forbidding murder. But He went on to explain that not only external acts of violence were sinful, but also internal anger or sharp and angry words. He did still more. He bound His followers to the practice of charity.

The Catholic Church has built on Christ's teaching a whole edifice of moral doctrine that touches every aspect of personal and social morality. Certain areas of this teaching have crucial importance today.

Abortion

No aspect of the Fifth Commandment is more crucial in the modern world than the morality of abortion. One reason is that the followers of Christ are now facing the same organized amorality as the Church struggled to Christianize in the first century. Historians of the Roman Empire in apostolic times say that infanticide was persistent, legal, and widely accepted; abortion was lawful for anyone who could obtain the means, and was very common not only among the well-to-do but among all classes.

It was in this atmosphere that Christ's teaching began to penetrate a pagan world. About the year 80 A.D. appeared *The Teaching of the Twelve Apostles*, the earliest Christian writing now known, outside of the canonical books of the New Testament, "There are two ways," the *Teaching* declared, "one of Life and one of Death."

> Now, the way of Life is this: first, love the God who made you; secondly, your neighbor as yourself; do not do to another what you do not wish to be done to yourself. . . .
>
> A further commandment of the Teaching: Do not murder . . . Do not kill a fetus by abortion, or commit infanticide.

Those who believed in Christ and accepted the Church's authority accepted the children whom God was sending them.

As Christianity pervaded human society, abortion became not only morally sinful but legally criminal according to civil law. There the matter stood until the twentieth century, when under pressure from the forces of secularism, one country after another legalized abortion. In many parts of the world, abortion has become a social custom, where it is the external manifestation of a people's decadence.

The Church's condemnation of abortion became part of the teaching of the Second Vatican Council.

> God, the Lord of life, has entrusted to man the noble mission of safeguarding life, and men must carry it out in a manner worthy of themselves. Life must be protected with the utmost care from the moment of conception: abortion

and infanticide are abominable crimes (*Constitution on the Church in the Modern World*, 51).

After the Council, Pope Paul VI ordered a detailed document to be published on procured abortion (*Declaration on Procured Abortion*, November 18, 1974). It is the longest and most detailed declaration on the subject in the Church's two-thousand years of moral history. It explains the evil of abortion in the light of faith, and in the additional light of reason; it replies to some of the widely circulated objections; it clarifies the relationship of morality, which comes from God, and civil law favoring abortion, which comes from men; and concludes that a Christian understanding of abortion cannot be limited to the horizon of this world. Only in the light of the world to come can sound moral judgments and rational human laws be made.

First the Roman document goes back over the Church's long and unanimous history in condemning abortion. Her tradition "has always held that human life must be protected and favored from the beginning, just as at the various stages of its development." Opposing the morals of the Greco-Roman world, the Church of the first centuries made a clear distinction between divine law and the world's law. From the beginning, the Church considered "as murderers, those women who took medicines to procure an abortion." She condemned "the killers of children, including those still living in their mother's womb, where they are already the object of the care of divine Providence" (6).

Catholic moral doctrine on this matter "has not changed and is not changeable." Those who arbitrarily discriminate on which innocent persons have a right to live are rationalizing murder.

The first right of a human person is his life. He has other goods and some are more precious, but this one is fundamental—the condition of all others. It does not belong to society, nor does it belong to public authority in any form to recognize this right for some and not for others. All discrimination is evil, whether it be founded on race, sex, color, or religion. It is not recognition by another that constitutes this right. This right is antecedent to its recognition; it demands recognition and it is strictly unjust to refuse it (11).

So much for the general principle which has been tragically ignored in the massive genocide of the twentieth century. Millions have already been murdered because of discrimination on "race, sex, color, or religion."

Now a new form of genocide has become legal in what still claim to be civilized countries. It is based on a discrimination of age or physical or psychological condition. This, too, is contrary to the divine laws.

Any discrimination in the various stages of life is no more justified than any other discrimination. The right to life remains complete in an old

259

person, even one greatly weakened; it is not lost by one who is incurably sick.

The right to life is no less to be respected in the small infant just born than in the mature person.

In reality, respect for human life is called for from the time that the process of generation begins. From the time that the ovum is fertilized, a life is begun which is neither that of the father nor of the mother. It is, rather, the life of a new human being with its own growth. It would never be made human if it were not human already (12).

Given the widespread legalization of direct abortion, with the intention to kill an unborn child, followers of Christ are placed in an agonizing dilemma. May they obey the civil law? No. "Man can never obey a law which is in itself immoral, and such is the case of a law which would admit, in principle, the licitness of abortion." May they argue from pluralism, that in a country with different religions, a Catholic should not impose his views on others, even if he is a legislator, judge, or holder of a political office? No. It is not imposition of Catholic views to oppose abortion: It is "obedience to the law of God." This law is based on "the natural law engraved in men's hearts by the Creator, as a norm which reason clarifies and strives to formulate properly, and which one must always struggle to understand better, but which it is always wrong to contradict" (21, 22, 24).

Euthanasia

It is not surprising that the foregoing declaration of Rome on abortion should soon after be followed by one on euthanasia.

The word *euthanasia* (Greek = easy death) is itself misleading. It has come to mean everything from murder of the unwanted to suicide by those who want to take their own lives—always with the approval and even coercion of the civil law.

As the Church understands the term, euthanasia is an action or an omission which, of itself or by intention, causes death. The motive for intending to kill an innocent person is not important. It may be to spare a person continued bodily suffering or to remove a disabled person from being a burden to himself or others, or to spare a mentally ill or incurably sick person from perhaps years of misery. No matter. These and other reasons for killing oneself or another innocent person do not justify what has been renamed "mercy killing" or "dying with dignity."

Certainly, physical and psychological suffering can be intense. It can be so severe as to arouse the desire to remove it at any cost. But Christianity teaches that suffering has a special place in God's plan of salvation. It is nothing less than a share in Christ's Passion and a union with His own redeeming sacrifice on Calvary.

Yet, there is nothing morally wrong in wanting to lessen the intensity of the pain and make it more tolerable. What may not be done, however, is to remove further suffering by directly intending to kill oneself or another person. God is Master of human life and its duration, not we.

The marvelous progress in medicine has extended the length of human life beyond anything in previous history. Life expectancy has been doubled in many countries in less than one century. The question now arises of what means may or must be used to prolong human life. The Church's answer has not changed, even as the developments of medical science have advanced phenomenally. We must use "ordinary" means to remain and keep others alive. Other terms are "normal" or "adequate" or "proportionate" means. Always it is understood that there is a sincere intention to stay alive or keep another person alive. There is no desire to kill in order to remove the suffering or the burden of continued living.

There are persons or situations where extraordinary means should be employed if they are available. Thus, when a person's continued life is extraordinarily necessary, even such means as are out of the ordinary are to be used.

The norms which the Church gives the faithful are based on reason and revelation. These norms were ordered by Pope John Paul II:

> Life is a gift of God, and on the other hand death is inevitable. It is necessary, therefore, that we, without in any way hastening the hour of death, should be able to accept it with full re-

sponsibility and dignity. It is true that death marks the end of our earthly existence, but at the same time it opens the door to eternal life (*Declaration on Euthanasia*, May 5, 1980).

As with abortion, so with euthanasia, the key to understanding the Church's moral doctrine is the fact that God, and He alone, is the final Master of human life and death.

Capital Punishment

The biblical warrant for capital punishment is given by St. Paul. "The State is there," he says, "to serve God for your benefit. If you break the law, however, you may well have fear; the bearing of the sword has its significance" (Romans 3:4).

The Church defends the death penalty imposed for the punishment of grave crimes. She bases her defense on the grounds of the common good. The State is like a body composed of many members. No less than a surgeon may cut off one diseased limb to save the others, so the civil authority may lawfully put a criminal to death and thus provide for the common good.

What bears emphasis is that capital punishment is lawful not only because it will deter others from committing the same crime. Capital punishment is also a punishment: Wrong has been done to society by a criminal. The State is divinely authorized to penalize the one who had been tried and found guilty of a serious crime.

However, the State itself is under the judgment of God. Totalitarian states that put to death political dissenters or, worse still, religious believers, are themselves guilty of crime before the Almighty.

War and Peace

Armed conflict between nations has been going on since the beginning of recorded history. In the Old Testament, the Israelites were often at war with their neighbors. And in one sweeping statement Job exclaimed that, "the life of man upon earth is a warfare" (Job 7:1).

One of the most appealing promises of the prophets was to predict that the Messiah would bring peace. On Christmas morning the angels sang, "Glory to God in the highest, and on earth peace to men of good will" (Luke 2:14).

During His public ministry, Christ said some surprising things about peace. He did not promise to end wars, nor assure His followers they would not experience conflict. He came to bring peace, indeed, but not as the world gives peace. His peace was to be bought through victory over self, the world, and the devil. His peace was to be the reward of submitting one's will to the will of God.

In the early Church there were some who held that no follower of Christ may engage in military service. But pacifism, or the claim that war is always sinful, has never been the mind of the Church's universal teaching authority. Catholic doctrine says that war is certainly undesirable and sinful passions give rise to war, but not all armed conflict is morally wrong, and Christians may engage in a just war.

Conditions for a Just War. St. Augustine was the first early Christian writer to give extensive attention to the conditions that would justify war. He said war may be undertaken for the good of society. His basic reason was that armed force is permitted when the purpose is to attain peace.

Since the sixteenth century, Catholic thinking, approved by Church authority, has come to identify the following reasons for a just war.

- It must be on the authority of the sovereign, that is, of the one (or ones) having supreme jurisdiction in the State.

- There must be a just cause: For example, the independence or vital possessions of the State are gravely threatened.

- Other means short of war have been sincerely tried but have failed.

- The belligerents must have a valid purpose, namely the advancement of some moral good or the avoidance of some evil.

- The war must be waged by proper means, since even a morally good end may not be sought by using means that are morally bad.

• There must be due proportion between the foreseeable benefits and the known evils that accompany war.

The rise of modern warfare with its massive destruction and the availability of nuclear weapons have made the Church speak out very plainly on the morality of war.

Popes Benedict XV, Pius XI, and Pius XII wrote extensively and urgently before and during the First and Second World Wars. Then the Second Vatican Council made the longest declaration on the subject of any ecumenical council in the Church's history.

Their teaching may be briefly stated in a series of moral principles:

1. Although war is not of its very nature morally evil, nuclear war is very difficult to justify in practice.

2. War that tends indiscriminately to destroy entire cities or wide areas with their inhabitants is a crime against God and man.

3. Those conscripted into military service may assume that their nation is right and engage in conflict.

4. Volunteers should seriously inquire whether their country's cause is a just one before they enter military service.

No single issue of modern life has been more urgently pleaded for than peace among nations. But peace between people depends on peace within people. Peace within persons is possible only if their wills are conformed to the will of God. Each individual contributes to world peace to the extent that he or she cooperates with divine grace in the depths of his own soul.

SIXTH AND NINTH COMMANDMENTS

In the Catholic version of the Decalogue, the Sixth and Ninth Commandments are coupled together. They both prescribe the practice of chastity.

The biblical text for the Sixth Commandment is simply "You shall not commit adultery" in both Exodus 20:14 and Deuteronomy 5:18. But the Ninth Commandment is part of a longer prohibition of covetousness.

> You shall not covet your neighbor's house. You shall not covet your neighbor's wife or his servant, man or woman, or his ox or his donkey, or anything that is his (Exodus 20:17).
> You shall not covet your neighbor's wife, you shall not set your heart on his house, his field, his servant—man or woman—or his ox or his donkey, or anything that is his (Deuteronomy 5:21).

There is a basic similarity in these two prohibitions, but Deuteronomy places the command "You shall not covet your neighbor's wife" first among the forms of greed which include property, cattle, and servants.

In pre-Christian Jewish morality, adultery rested on the idea that a wife was the property of the husband. Strictly speaking,, therefore, only the husband's rights could be violated. Illicit intercourse was not really adultery if the woman was not married. Thus a wife and her partner could violate the rights of her husband, but the husband could not violate the rights of his wife. She had no marital rights to violate.

Old Testament morality forbade adultery both in act and in desire. But in both cases it was essentially a sin of injustice, along with stealing or coveting other possessions that a man might own.

New Testament Teaching

Jesus repeated the Sixth and Ninth Commandments but He elevated them in a way that has been the single most demanding precept of the New Law. His teaching is found in the Synoptic Gospels of Matthew, Mark, and Luke. St. Paul adds a great deal to the gospel narratives, so that the New Testament revelation on chastity is extraordinarily complete.

Unity and Indissolubility of Marriage. The heart of the Savior's doctrine on marital unity and indissolubility occurs in a dialogue He had with the Pharisees. They asked him if a man could put away his wife for any reason. This was meant to trap Jesus into taking sides with either the strict rabbis, who allowed divorce and remarriage only for adultery, or the liberal rabbis, who allowed it on any pretext whatever.

Instead of taking sides Jesus reminded the Pharisees that at the beginning of the human race, there was no divorce with the right to remarry. "So then," He concluded, "what God has united, man must not divide." To which the Pharisees objected that Moses permitted divorce and remarriage. Christ answered, "It was because you were so unteachable." He then concluded, "The man who divorces his wife—I am not speaking of fornication—and marries another, is guilty of adultery" (Matthew 19:3–9).

What Christ meant by the phrase, "I am not speaking of fornication," was that infidelity would justify a divorce, but not remarriage. This is plain from the parallel texts in St. Mark (10:2–12), St. Luke (16:18), and St. Paul (I Corinthians 7:10–39; Romans 7:2–3). St. Mark, a disciple of St. Peter, writing for converts from paganism, further mentions Christ's saying that "if a woman divorces her husband and marries another she is guilty of adultery too" (Mark 10:12).

Jesus here elevated the Old Law by completely abrogating the practice of remarriage after divorce, which had been merely tolerated in the Mosaic Law.

Internal Chastity. Only St. Matthew records the Master's further raising the morality of the Decalogue. The Old Testament condemned the act of adultery and the sin of coveting another man's wife. But it considered internal adultery a sin of injustice.

It did not precisely identify it as a sin against the virtue of temperance.

The difference between the two is important. To desire what belongs to someone else is wrong because it denies another person's rights to what he or she possesses. But to desire what God forbids me to enjoy is wrong because it denies His right to tell me how I am to use my faculties of body and soul. The full text in St. Matthew should be quoted.

> You have heard it was said "You must not commit adultery." But I say this to you: If a man looks at a woman lustfully, He has already committed adultery with her in his heart. If your right eye should cause you to sin, tear it out and throw it away; for it will do you less harm to lose one part of you than to have your whole body thrown into hell (Matthew 5:27–29).

Words could not be plainer. What the Catholic Church calls the Ninth Commandment forbids all lustful thoughts and desires. Pope John Paul II observed that this precept of Christ applies equally to men and women: Both genders must control their sexual desires. To control these desires requires practicing custody of all the senses, but especially of the eyes and touch.

Consecrated Chastity. The capstone of Jesus' teaching on chastity occurs in the context of His restoring marriage to its original form of monogamy.

He had just told the Pharisees that a man commits adultery if he puts away his wife and remarries:

> The disciples said to Him, "If that is how things are between husband and wife, it is not advisable to marry." But He replied, "It is not everyone who can accept what I have said, but only to those to whom it is granted. There are eunuchs born that way from their mother's womb, there are eunuchs made so by men, and there are eunuchs who have made themselves that way for the sake of the kingdom of heaven. Let those accept this who can" (Matthew 19:10–12).

Since apostolic times there have been men and women who did accept this teaching and who believed they had the necessary grace to sacrifice marriage "for the sake of the kingdom of heaven."

The Church distinguishes two levels of God's will in our regard. There are precepts binding on everyone under pain of sin; and there are counsels, inviting those who have the grace to do more for God.

Holiness is available to all followers of Christ in every state of life. And holiness, says the Second Vatican Council, "is fostered in a special way by the manifold counsels which the Lord proposes to His disciples in the gospel for them to observe." This is where the counsel of dedicated chastity is part of God's mysterious Providence.

> Towering among these counsels is that precious gift of divine grace given to some by the

Father to devote themselves to God alone more easily with an undivided heart in virginity or celibacy. This perfect continence for love of the kingdom of heaven has always been held in high esteem by the Church as a sign and stimulus of love, and as a singular source of spiritual fertility in the world (*Constitution on the Church*, V, 42).

The adverb "always" in the foregoing statement is proved by the Church's history. Sacrifice of the experience of marriage has been part of Catholic Christianity since Christ set the pattern for His disciples.

Observance of Chastity

We see that there are three forms of chastity recognized by the Catholic Church. They may be called marital chastity, unmarried chastity, and consecrated chastity. Each has its own responsibilities and corresponding legislation by Church authority.

Marital chastity requires that husband and wife remain faithful to each other. It further requires that they do not deliberately interfere with the divinely ordained purpose of marital intercourse, which is the conception of a new human being.

Unmarried chastity requires that a person never deliberately arouses sexual pleasure, or willfully consents to the pleasure once it is aroused.

By assuming a life of perfect continence followers of Christ make the sacrifice of seeking marriage.

They voluntarily give up what other unmarried persons may lawfully and laudably desire.

On all three levels the faithful practice of chastity is more than unaided human nature can accomplish. It calls for not only prayer but the spirit of prayer, which seeks to live in the presence of God. It requires the grace available through the sacraments of Penance and the Holy Eucharist. It demands watchful control of the senses. It exacts constant vigilance over the emotions and the imagination. And it must be built on a sincere humility, which has no illusions about one's own strength but relies on the power of God.

Sins of Unchastity

Chastity, it is said, takes its name from the fact that reason enlightened by faith, chastises concupiscence. Since concupiscence is the irrational desire of our fallen human nature, it needs to be curbed.

Among our irrational desires is the urge for sexual pleasure outside of marriage. And even in marriage, the sex drive needs to be constantly restrained.

Failure to control sexual desires goes by the general name of unchastity. But immediately we should distinguish two different kinds of unchastity. They are given different names depending on whether in sinning, nature's purpose of sex can be attained, or whether this purpose is frustrated. If the purpose is attainable, they are called natural sins against chastity. Otherwise the sins are said to be unnatural.

Fornication and Adultery. There are two principal so-called natural sins against chastity, namely fornication and adultery. In both cases conception can take place and a child can be born. In that sense the sins are "natural." But they are grave sins.

In fornication there is voluntary sexual intercourse between unmarried persons who are not bound by celibacy or a vow of consecrated chastity. If the persons are closely related to one another by blood, there is the further sin of incest. If either is under dedicated celibacy or chastity, they also commit a sacrilege.

The sinfulness of fornication lies in several facts. Those who indulge in sexual intercourse outside of marriage sin by injustice against each other. Neither partner has the loving and lifetime commitment that only marriage can provide. If they are baptized, neither has the divine blessing and supernatural grace assured by the sacrament of Matrimony. If a child is conceived and born, it does not have the security, stability, and selfless care that only a married father and mother can give. And society is destabilized by the bad example that fornication gives to others, especially the young. The basis of civilized society is shaken because the foundation of a sound society is a dedicated family, whereas by definition those indulging in fornication are not dedicated to each other by a permanent marriage bond.

Adultery is sexual intercourse with the husband or wife of a third person. Its sinfulness includes all the evils we have just seen in fornication, and others besides. Those who commit adultery, sin gravely against the rights of the husband or wife to whom they are married. The literature of all nations is filled with accounts of what adultery does to once happily married spouses. Murders and suicides have been provoked, even wars have been fought to avenge the crime of adultery. Not a small degree of emotional disturbance and mental breakdown can be traced to the crushing impact on the human personality caused by the adulterous behavior of a once devoted spouse.

Masturbation, Contraception and Homosexuality. The unnatural sins of unchastity are against the divinely ordained nature of sexual intercourse, which is to reproduce the human race.

Masturbation is the deliberate arousal of sexual pleasure caused by some form of self-stimulation. It is also called self-abuse, and is gravely sinful when fully conscious and indulged with full consent of the will.

Contraception is any action deliberately taken before, during, or after intercourse to prevent conception or fetal development. Contraception is gravely sinful because it contradicts the divinely intended purpose of marital intercourse, which is to foster procreative love.

As with abortion, so contraception has been consistently condemned by the Catholic Church from her earliest history. When Pope Paul VI published *Humanae vitae* (July 25, 1968), he stated that "the teaching of the Church on the regulation of birth" simply "promulgates the divine law." This law is first of all the law of nature which can be recognized by the light of reason. One of the most compelling reasons against contraception is the record of history. *Humanae vitae* gives some of the known and predictable results of contraception.

- The road is opened to conjugal infidelity and to the general lowering of morality.

- Men tend to lose respect for their wives, no longer caring for their physical and psychological welfare.

- Men tend to look on their wives as mere instruments of selfish enjoyment.

- Men tend no longer to look on their wives as beloved companions.

Given the widespread practice of contraception, some have questioned whether the Church's teaching on this grave moral issue is open to change. Pope Pius XI took issue with these dissenters in the clearest possible terms:

Openly departing from the uninterrupted Christian tradition, some recently have judged it possible solemnly to declare another doctrine on this question. . . .

The Catholic Church, to whom God has entrusted the defense and purity of morals, standing erect in the midst of the moral ruin which surrounds her, in order that she may preserve the chastity of the marital union from being defiled by this foul stain, raises her voice in token of divine Ambassadorship and through Our mouth proclaims anew: Any use whatsoever of matrimony exercised in such a way that the act is deliberately frustrated in its natural power to generate life is an offense against the law of God and of nature, and those who indulge in such are branded with the guilt of a grave sin (*Casti Connubii*, December 31, 1930).

Such will therefore always be the teaching of the Catholic Church. Her doctrine on contraception is irreversible.

One form of contraception that is becoming widespread is direct sterilization. This means that the body is deliberately deprived, either temporarily or permanently, of its power to beget or to bear children. The morality of contraceptive sterilization is to be judged in the same way as artificial birth control or contraception.

Homosexuality is any form of sexual relationship among persons of the same sex. A homosexual tendency is within the normal range of any human being. Given our fallen human nature, such a tendency is not unusual but must be recognized for what it is, contrary to divine law.

Homosexual attraction may be due to an individual's personality. More often, it is the result of indiscretion or seduction. Not sinful by itself, the sexual attraction must be resisted.

Homosexual activity is the result of voluntarily giving in to the tendency or attraction. It is gravely sinful and has been explicitly condemned in Sacred

Scripture. St. Paul describes the pagans of his day as having refused to honor God:

> That is why God has abandoned them to degrading passions: why their women have turned from natural intercourse to unnatural practices and why their menfolk have given up natural intercourse to be consumed with passion for each other, men doing shameless things with men and getting an appropriate reward for their perversion (Romans 1:26–27).

Historians of the Roman Empire in St. Paul's day testify to the fact that homosexual vice had sunk into a state of extreme laxity. In the apostle's words, "since they refused to see it as rational to acknowledge God, God has left them to their own irrational ideas and to their monstrous behavior" (Romans 1:28).

There is a tragic logic in the relation between indifference to God and sexual immorality. Those who refuse to bend their minds in the humble worship of God do not receive the grace to keep their passions under rational control.

Natural Family Planning

Already in apostolic times, husbands and wives would abstain from marital relations "only for an agreed time, to leave yourselves free for prayer" (I Corinthians 7:1, 4–5).

With the rise of a contraceptive mentality in modern times, the Church has more than once returned to the subject of periodic continence or, as it is popularly called, natural family planning. On Catholic moral principles, a couple may for a good reason abstain from intercourse during the wife's fertile periods. Married people, the Church tells them, may "renounce the use of marriage when for just motives, procreation is not desirable. They make use of it during the sterile periods to manifest their affection and to safeguard their mutual fidelity. By so doing, they give proof of a truly and fully praiseworthy love" (Paul VI, *Humanae vitae,* II, 16).

This is morally permissible, and oftentimes commendable because there is no interference with the purpose of marital intercourse. It is rather, in the Church's language, making legitimate use of a disposition provided by the Author of nature.

SEVENTH AND TENTH
COMMANDMENTS

The biblical precept of the Seventh Commandment, like the Sixth, is a short imperative, "You shall not steal." It is the same in both versions of the Decalogue. The Tenth Commandment, as already seen, is that part of the Ten Commandments which forbids coveting what belongs to someone else, whether his house, servant, ox, donkey, or anything else. Deuteronomy distinguishes between coveting "your neighbor's wife," and "setting your heart" on other possessions, including the neighbor's field (Exodus 20:15; Deuteronomy 5:19).

Like the Sixth and Ninth Commandments, the Seventh and Tenth not only forbid actually taking another person's property, but even internally desiring to appropriate it. The reason for both prohibitions is obvious. Before God, sin consists in the will acting contrary to the will of God. There would be no stealing with the hands if there had not first been stealing with the heart.

Christ repeated the Seventh Commandment not to steal (Mark 10:19). He also repeated the frequent

Old Testament prohibition of fraud. But once again He elevated the Mosaic Law far above what it had been before God became man to teach human beings how to reach heaven. The Church has built on the gospel and developed a profound morality of ownership and poverty that has literally changed the face of the earth.

Control of Covetousness

If there is one thing that Christ brought out plainly it is that human society has inequality. Some people have more of this world's goods than others.

If we look more closely at the reason for this inequality, we find it is due to various causes.

- God simply gives some people more than others.

- Some people are more enterprising and energetic than others.

- There is injustice among human beings. Depriving others of what they deserve, preventing them from obtaining even what they need, exploiting the work and talents of others, and outright stealing—are all notorious forms of injustice that have become part of world history.

There is such a thing as recognizing inequality and not allowing it to dominate our thoughts. Otherwise, what others have can become the source of envy. Envy in turn can change covetousness into greed, and greed then leads to all kinds of sin.

The secret of keeping the Seventh Commandment is to observe the Tenth. Either we master our minds from comparing what others have and what we lack, or our hands will seek to appropriate other people's possessions.

Poverty of Detachment

Time and again Christ preached the need for internal detachment from material possessions. His conversation with a man who felt he was being cheated is typical:

> A man in the crowd said to Him, "Master tell my brother to give me a share of our inheritance." "My friend," He replied, "who appointed me your judge or the arbitor of your claims?" Then He said to them, "Watch and be on your guard against avarice of any kind, for a man's life is not made secure by what he owns even when he has more than he needs" (Luke 12:13–15).

Internal poverty of detachment, as proclaimed by Christ, goes beyond the avoidance of covetousness taught in the Decalogue. Detachment means not only not coveting what belongs to someone else: It means not coveting any earthly possession, period. In Christ's language we are not to set our hearts on any temporal goods, no matter how lawfully acquired.

283

Our hearts should be set on the treasures of heaven, where neither moth consumes nor thieves can break in and steal.

Detachment is to be practiced by all who call themselves Christian, the rich and the poor alike. Those who are rich are to be detached by not being proud, and by sharing their possessions with those who are poor. Those who are poor are to be detached by not envying or worse still, hating those who are rich.

Christ's focus in treating of earthly wealth was on eternity. He kept telling His followers to set their sights on the Horizon beyond this life, and not to allow preoccupation with material things to blind them to the true riches of the spirit. The body will die, but the soul lives on. It is sheer wisdom to accumulate the spiritual treasures of grace and virtue that have lasting value beyond the limitations of space and time.

The Savior spoke of money. He did not deny its use in this world. He even told the disciples: "Use money, tainted as it is, to win you friends, and thus make sure that when it fails you, they will welcome you into the tents of eternity." But He immediately qualified. Money has to be used, yet in such a way that it does not become our master. "You cannot be the slave of both God and money" (Luke 16:9–13).

This is the central theme of Christ's message about material goods. We must keep our hearts from being enslaved by any creature. We must be "enslaved" only to the Creator.

Stealing and Restitution

There are several words that mean almost the same thing, but they are somewhat different.

- "Theft" is the most general term for taking what belongs to someone else, without the owner's consent.

- "Stealing" is theft but implies that something is taken secretly and not only without the owner's permission, but without his knowledge.

- "Robbery" is also theft, but violence or intimidation is used to force the owner to give up what he possesses.

- "Burglary" is again theft but committed in such a way that the thief breaks in on the owner's premises or property with the intention to steal.

- "Larceny" is theft in which someone's property is removed from the place where it belongs in order to be appropriated by the thief.

Other terms are also used, and the laws of all nations are filled with a variety of terms for unlawfully taking someone else's property. Evidently the Seventh Commandment is frequently broken by many people.

What is less clear is that "property cries out for

its owner." What has been stolen never really becomes owned by the thief. It belongs to its original possessor, no matter how much or how little the stolen object may be, and no matter how long a time may have elapsed since the thieving took place.

Always implied is that the owner wants back what was taken; that the stolen object is precious to him; and that he is reasonable in his unwillingness to give up the ownership of what justly belongs to him.

Restitution, therefore, of the stolen goods is an obligation that follows naturally on stealing. The seriousness of restitution depends on the value of what was stolen; on the desire of the owner to have his property restored; and on the practical difficulty—or even possibility—of restoring the stolen material.

So important is restitution, that the willingness to restore what was stolen, or its equivalent, is a condition for having the sin of theft forgiven by God.

Cheating and Gambling

There are numerous forms of cheating. In general, to cheat is to deceive by trickery or fraud to gain something a person wants. People can cheat to obtain academic credit or a degree in school, or employment, or recognition, or social standing. For our purpose, cheating is a form of stealing to obtain something of material value like property or money. The means used are always some kind of fraud.

Cheating is always sinful, in fact twice over; once for using deceit to obtain something and once again for depriving another person or even others of what belongs to them. As with stealing, cheating calls for restitution.

In a class by itself is gambling, which the Catholic Church does not consider sinful by itself. To gamble is to stake money or some other valuable on chance, or a future event that is unknown or uncertain to those who take part.

Gambling was commonly practiced in pagan Rome. On Calvary after the soldiers had crucified Christ they decided to gamble on who would get the Savior's seamless garment: " 'Let's throw dice,' " they said to one another, " 'to decide who is to have it.' " In this way the words of Scripture were fulfilled, " 'They cast lots for my clothes.' This is exactly what the soldiers did" (John 19:24).

But then we hear that after Christ's ascension Peter told the other ten apostles they should choose someone who had known the Savior to replace the traitor Judas. There were two leading candidates. So "they drew lots for them and as the lot fell to Matthias, he was listed as one of the twelve apostles." It was assumed that having asked God to "show us which of these two you have chosen," the choice of Matthias by lot was really by divine inspiration (Acts 1:25–26).

Yet gambling and wagering can be even seriously sinful. When the gambler's resources are exposed to such loss as to gravely harm his dependents or himself, when gambling involves dishonesty, or weakens human society—it is contrary to the will of God. Experience shows that gambling can become an addic-

287

tion, in which case a person should simply give up gambling altogether.

Social Justice

One of the features of the modern world is its gradual lessening of space and time as a result of the communications revolution. In this sense, the Second Vatican Council was the first general council of the Catholic Church in modern times. One of the strongest imperatives of Vatican II is the duty to practice social justice.

Broadly defined, social justice is the virtue that enables us to cooperate with other people in developing a society whose laws and institutions better serve the common good.

Each person must, of course, do his own part in the practice of this virtue. But the very nature of society requires that individuals work together with others through organized bodies. Otherwise the good achieved will be minimal, and the presence of alien forces may neutralize even the most zealous efforts to practice the works of mercy.

Three passages from three modern popes point up the serious, even desperate need for social justice to be practiced according to the norms of Catholic Christianity.

The rise of Communism is a warning to Christians to work for a more just distribution of the material possessions of the earth.

Then only will the economic and social order be soundly established . . . when it offers to all . . . all those goods which the wealth and resources of nature, technical science, and the corporate organization of social affairs can give (Pius XI, Encyclical on *Atheistic Communism* 52).

There is a right to private ownership that stems from the natural law. And Marxism, which denies this right, is a philosophy that ignores the spontaneous desire of every person to possess and acquire something as one's own. But this natural desire may not deny or minimize the social and public character of ownership.

Private property does not give anyone an absolute and unconditional right [of ownership]. No one is justified in keeping for his exclusive use what he does not need, when others are lacking the necessities of life (Paul VI, Encyclical *Populorum progressio,* 22–24).

One more aspect of social justice is crucial. Whatever else Christ did, He elevated the virtue of altruism from the practice of justice to the highest form of charity.

Whereas justice respects the rights of others and does not enrich oneself by depriving another, charity deprives oneself to enrich another. Where justice asks: What may I not take away from another? charity asks: What does another person need that I can give?

289

So many social reformers urge that justice be practiced, but they forget that justice alone is not enough. In fact, in the name of justice the worst kind of injustice can be done.

> Very often programs which start from the idea of justice . . . in practice suffer from distortions, although they appeal to the idea of justice. Nevertheless experience shows that other negative forces have gained the upper hand over justice. Such are spite, hatred and even cruelty . . . The experience of the past and of our own time shows that justice alone is not enough. It can even lead to the destruction of itself, if that deeper power which is love, is not allowed to shape human life (John Paul II, Encyclical *Redemptor hominis*, 12).

St. Paul's praise of charity was not romantic poetry when he wrote that: "Love is always patient and kind; it is never jealous; love is never boastful or conceited; it is never rude or selfish" (I Corinthians 13:4–5). Justice by itself can be very impatient and unkind, jealous, boastful and conceited, rude and profoundly selfish. This is not surprising once we realize that God had to become man to teach us the difference between not stealing, which is justice, and giving, which is love.

EIGHTH COMMANDMENT

In both versions of the Decalogue, the wording of the Eighth Commandment is the same: "You shall not bear false witness against your neighbor" (Exodus 20:16; Deuteronomy 5:20).

Throughout the Old Testament, the full meaning of this commandment includes both the prohibition against telling a lie and the precept of telling the truth. Thus, "Lips that tell the truth abide firm forever; the tongue that lies lasts only for a moment. Lips that lie are abhorrent to Yahweh; dear to Him those who speak the truth" (Proverbs 12:19, 19:22).

The Incarnation gave new depth to the Mosaic Law. Since Christ is Truth incarnate, He revealed truths that had never been known before. He also commanded His followers to proclaim these truths to the whole world until the end of time.

Obligation to Tell the Truth

Truth is the agreement of mind with reality. When what is in my mind agrees with what is outside my mind, I have the truth. Thus the existence of God is real. He really exists. When my mind knows this, I possess the truth. Again, there is a real earth of land and sea. When my mind knows this, I possess the truth. And so on regarding everything in existence. If what is on my mind inside of me corresponds to any reality outside of me, I have the truth. This kind of truth is called logical (Greek *logos* = mind) or mental truth.

There is another kind of truth called moral truth. This is the agreement of my speech, or what I say, with what is on my mind. So when I know something and I tell someone else what I know, I am telling the truth. However, if what I say disagrees with what I know, I am not telling the truth. And if I deliberately contradict in words what is on my mind, I am telling a lie. The simplest definition of a lie, therefore, is speech contrary to the mind.

We are forbidden by the natural and revealed law of God to speak, write, or in any other way communicate to others what is contrary to what we have in mind.

Consequently a lie is evil of its very nature. It can never be justified, for several reasons:

1. The divinely given power of speech is to enable us to share our thoughts with others, and

they with us. To lie is to use the faculty of communication contrary to its divinely intended purpose.

2. The natural function of human conversation is to share. When others speak to us, we assume they are telling the truth. When we speak to others, they assume the same of us.

3. If the person who listens is not told the truth, he or she is being deceived. It is a sin of injustice to tell a lie. Everyone has a right to hear the truth whenever anyone speaks. We may not want to say anything, and our silence may be justified. But if we speak, we must tell the truth.

4. Every lie is an injury to the one lying. He is damaged in his own personal integrity, and he loses the respect of others, once they find out he did not tell the truth.

5. Human society is built on the mutual trust between people. Lying breaks down this mutual trust and weakens the bond of unity. This bond of unity is the truth possessed by each individual person and shared among those who belong to the human race.

6. We can only love what we know and whom we know. How can we know others, to love them, unless they reveal themselves in the deepest part of their being—which is their mind? And how can others know us, unless we reveal ourselves by telling the truth?

Keeping Secrets

A secret is the knowledge of something that may not be made known to others, or may be shared in confidence with only a few. Keeping secrets is part of human existence in society and has been recognized since the dawn of recorded history.

A natural secret must be observed by reason of the natural law. Thus, if the disclosure of something known would do harm or displease another, it should not be disclosed. A good general rule is that if there are things about myself that I would not want others to know, I should keep them secret from another person. Past sins committed, weaknesses of character, embarrassing information about someone's family, humiliating mistakes made, illegitimacy, unpaid debts, past history of expulsion from school—are examples of natural secrets. Depending on the seriousness of the matter, natural secrets may bind under mortal sin.

A promised secret is one that a person agrees to keep after some confidential knowledge has been received. It is assumed that there is no opportunity beforehand to decline receiving some secret information. Promised secrets normally oblige under venial sin.

An entrusted secret is obtained only on condition that the confidence will be kept; otherwise the information would not have been given. The promise in an entrusted secret may be explicit when I am formally asked beforehand to keep something confidential, and I agree. Or the promise may be implicit, as in the case of professional persons, like lawyers, physicians, counselors, religious superiors, or civil officials; they receive information from people who assume that their confidences will not be betrayed. It is not permitted to reveal secret knowledge unless there is a grave reason. Such would be serious harm to the one who has the secret knowledge, or to the person about whom something confidential is known, or to a third person, or to society in general. Entrusted or professional secrets are the most sacred, outside the seal of confession.

The seal of confession may never be broken under any circumstances. What is heard in confession binds the confessor absolutely. It also binds anyone who discovers what is confessed, unless it is freely revealed by the penitent outside of confession.

Canon Law has several provisions covering the seal of confession.

The sacramental seal is inviolable. Accordingly, it is absolutely wrong for a confessor in any way to betray the penitent, for any reason whatsoever, whether by word or in any other fashion. . . .

An interpreter, if there is one, is also obliged to observe this secret, as are all others who in any way whatever have come to a knowledge of sins from confession (Canon 983).

The confessor is wholly forbidden to use knowledge acquired in confession to the detriment of the penitent, even when all danger of disclosure is excluded. . . .

A person who is in authority may not in any way, for the purpose of external governance, use knowledge about sins which has at any time come to him from the hearing of confession (Canon 984).

The penalty for directly violating the seal of confession, by identifying penitent and sin confessed, is an automatic excommunication. Only the Holy See can remove the excommunication (Canon 1388).

Mental Reservation

We may never tell a lie. But we are also obliged to keep secrets. How to resolve the dilemma? An approved way is by what is called mental reservation.

A legitimate mental reservation is to reserve in one's mind the real meaning of what is said, but allow the listener a reasonable clue that such reservation is being made. If a prudent person can gather the intended meaning from the circumstances, then it is a broad mental reservation. Broad mental reservations are not only permissible but may be obligatory.

A strict mental reservation provides no reasonable clue to the real meaning of what is said. Actually strict mental reservations are lies.

Defamation of Character

Good esteem is the opinion which people have about someone's excellence. We all naturally want to be well thought of by others, and others want to be well thought of by us.

Defamation is the injury by word or actions done to a person's reputation or good esteem. There are, in general, two forms of defamation, namely, detraction and calumny. Both are sinful and gravely wrong when serious injury is done to a person's reputation.

In detraction, what is said about another person is true, but there was no real need to make the disclosure that harms the person's good name. Detraction becomes slander when done maliciously.

In calumny, what defames another's reputation is not true. Calumny is therefore sinful both as lying and as an act of injustice to someone, because of the undeserved harm done to the person's esteem in the minds of others.

Judging Others

The New Testament has some strong language about judging other people. "Be compassionate about judging other people," Christ tells us, "as your Father is compassionate. Do not judge and you will not be judged yourselves" (Luke 6:36–37).

Because this is so practically important, it should be carefully explained. We must immediately distinguish two kinds of judgments we can make about people. We can judge the morality of the actions, and we can judge the morality of the persons.

We have to judge whether a given action is objectively good or bad. If I see someone stealing or hear someone cursing, or know that someone is unfaithful to his or her married spouse, I spontaneously and justifiably recognize that such conduct is morally wrong.

But when I move from the external action to a person's internal responsibility for the action, I must pause. I may not make a rash judgment. A rash judgment would be made if I concluded, without strong evidence, that the person is guilty for doing something wrong. Finally, only God can read the human heart. Only He knows for certain whether and how culpable people are when they commit what is objectively sinful.

Social Communications

The rise of the modern media—print, film, radio, recording, television, and computer—have created moral issues that are deeply affecting the whole human race.

First we must state the basic principle: Only the truth may be communicated by the media. Therefore the first duty of those who use the media is to tell the truth. Lying is sinful whether done by one person to another, or done through the media that reach millions of readers, viewers, or listeners.

Consequently the main condition for the right use of the media is that those who control the media are willing to follow sound moral principles.

These principles begin with the obvious one of telling the truth. But there are other norms besides:

1. The media must be concerned to advance the common good of society and not only of some aggressive special interest group.

2. The ideas and information communicated must be within the limits of justice and charity.

3. There should be a wise balance between what is true, useful, and also personally appealing.

Among the areas that constantly reflect the Eighth Commandment is the field of advertising. The purpose of advertising is to sell or promote what is being advertised. Advertising is not only beneficial but necessary in the modern world. But it must be controlled by certain moral norms. Among these are especially the use of morally good means and the promotion of morally good products, services, or personalities.

One postconciliar statement of the Holy See brings out the gravity of the moral issues involved: "People can get the impression that the instruments of communication exist solely to stimulate man's appetites so that these can be satisfied later by the acquisition of the thing advertised" *(Communio et progressio,* 59).

The Catholic Church's right to use the modern

media for proclaiming the true faith and sound morality rests on the mandate she has received from her Founder. That is why the Second Vatican Council did not hesitate to declare: "It is the Church's birthright to use and own any of these media for the formation of Christians and for pastoral activity (*Decree on the Means of Social Communication,* 3).

The Catholic Church believes that Christ entrusted to her the fullness of divine revelation. She therefore realizes that the use of the media for evangelization and religious instruction is not an option but a serious moral obligation.

PART FOUR

LORD, TEACH US TO PRAY

THE LORD'S PRAYER

By every standard of comparison, the most popular prayer in existence is the Our Father. One sign of its popularity is the number of polyglot collections of the Lord's Prayer which have been published at various times since the invention of printing. Already in 1787 the Spaniard Hervaz printed the *Pater Noster* in three hundred and seven dialects and languages, and the practice of multi-lingual editions has been going on ever since.

But the Lord's Prayer is not only the most popular prayer in existence, it is also the most important. According to St. Augustine, "whatever else we say when we pray, if we pray as we should, we are only saying what is already contained in the Lord's Prayer" (*Letter* 121, 12).

The recitation of the Lord's Prayer has been woven into the fabric of popular devotion since the days of the catacombs. It forms part of the Divine Office and has been so closely associated with the Sacrifice of the Mass that some have mistakenly thought that without the *Pater Noster* there would be no valid consecration of the Holy Eucharist.

One more reflection: If the Our Father is so popular and so important, is it also the perfect model of what all our prayers should be? Yes. One Father and Doctor of the Church after another—Saints Cyprian and Augustine, Teresa of Avila and Robert Bellarmine—did not hesitate to say that the Lord's Prayer is the divinely revealed pattern of what all Christian prayers should be.

Brevity and Scope

The brevity of the Our Father is remarkable, because the number of its petitions could hardly be shorter and yet more exalted. The special merit of this brevity is that it can be easily memorized. Since the early days of the Church, those preparing for baptism were expected to recite the Lord's Prayer by heart.

Moreover, we are thereby reminded that there is no need of much talking when we pray. Why not? Because we are speaking to God who knows what we need before we ask Him. What is more important is the devotion and fervor of spirit with which we pray.

The masters of the spiritual life found in the Our Father a proof of the wisdom of Christ, who compressed into a few words all the desires and aspirations of the human heart in its intimate communication with God.

Perfection of the Lord's Prayer

Among the many saintly commentators on the Lord's Prayer, St. Thomas Aquinas explains why it must be the most perfect prayer that we can say.

The *Pater Noster* was taught us by Christ Himself. It was also the only prayer He taught us to say. And He gave it to us in answer to the request of His disciples, "Lord, teach us to pray" (Luke 11:1).

However, what makes it also commendable is that the structure of the Our Father is perfect.

Since prayer is an interpretation of our desires, we should only pray for those things which are proper for us to desire. . . .

Now in the Lord's Prayer what we are asking for from God is everything that we may lawfully ambition. It is, therefore, not only a catalogue of petitions but also, and especially, a corrective for our affections. . . .

Thus the first object of our desires is our last end; then the means to arrive at this end. But our end is God, to whom our affections incline in two ways: the one in desiring the glory of God, the other in wishing to enjoy this divine glory. The first belongs to charity by which we love God in Himself; the second to charity by which we love ourselves in God. So, the first petition, "Hallowed be Thy name," asks for the glory of God; and the

305

second, "Thy Kingdom come," asks that we may come to the enjoyment of this glory. . . .

Moreover, we are directed to the end of our existence either by something which is essential or by something which is accidental as a means of salvation. But, it can be essential again either directly, according to the merit by which we deserve beatitude because we are obedient to God, and in this sense we ask: "Thy will be done on earth as it is in heaven"; or it may be only instrumental, although essential, because it helps us to merit heaven. And in this respect we say: "Give us this day our daily bread," whether we understand this of the sacramental bread of the Eucharist, the daily use of which is profitable to salvation, or of the bread of the body, which is symbolic for a sufficiency of food. . . .

We are also directed to heaven, accidentally, by the removal of obstacles to beatitude; 1) sin, which directly excludes man from the kingdom of God. Therefore, we pray "Forgive us our trespasses"; 2) temptation, which leads us into sin. Hence our sixth petition, "Lead us not into temptation"; 3) temporal evils, the consequence of sin, which make the burden of life too heavy. Consequently, our final petition, "Deliver us from evil" (*Summa Theologica*, II, II, 83).

Centuries before St. Thomas and ever since, theologians and mystics, exegetes and moralists have written extensively and in depth, explaining the seven petitions of the Lord's Prayer and applying its lessons to our daily lives.

Words of the Our Father

There are two versions of the Our Father in the gospels. The longer version is in St. Matthew's Gospel, where it forms part of Christ's Sermon on the Mount. The Lord is explaining how we should pray, and warns His disciples not to multiply words, as the Gentiles do. They think that by talking a great deal, they will be heard. Christians are not to pray in this way. Why not? Because God already knows what we need before we ask Him. "In this manner therefore shall you pray:

> Our Father, who art in heaven, hallowed be Thy Name.
> Thy Kingdom come, Thy will be done on earth as it is in heaven.
> Give us this day our daily bread.
> And forgive us our debts, as we also forgive our debtors.
> And lead us not into temptation.
> But deliver us from evil. Amen" (Matthew 6:9–15).

The foregoing is the text in the Latin Vulgate of the New Testament.

Already in apostolic times, the *Pater Noster* was part of the Eucharistic Liturgy, where it was followed by the words, "For thine is the power and the glory, for evermore." This ending occurs in the first-century liturgical manual, *The Teaching of the Twelve Apostles* (8:2). It was taken over by the Eastern Liturgy of St. John Chrysostom and may be found in some gospel manuscripts. Since the Second Vatican Council, the liturgical addition called the embolism is part of the Eucharistic Prayer in the Latin Rite.

In St. Luke's Gospel, the Lord's Prayer occurs as part of the narrative in which the disciples find Jesus praying in a certain place. After He has finished praying, one of the disciples asks Him, "Lord, teach us to pray, even as John also taught his disciples." He told them, "When you pray, say:

Father, hallowed be Thy Name. Thy Kingdom come.

Give us this day our daily bread.

And forgive us our sins, for we also forgive every one who is indebted to us.

And lead us not into temptation" (Luke 11:2–4).

The Church has adopted St. Matthew's text for the liturgy and for its daily use by the faithful.

THE INVOCATION: "OUR FATHER, WHO ART IN HEAVEN"

We open the Lord's Prayer by addressing God as Father. The *Pater Noster* is addressed to the Holy Trinity, Father, Son, and Holy Spirit. But we speak to Him as Father because God is our Father by every possible title.

- He is our Father because He is our Creator, who brought us into existence out of nothing.

- He is our Father because He is our Redeemer and therefore the source of our supernatural life.

- He is our Father because we are His children by adoption, sharing already on earth in His own divine life by the grace He has given us.

- He is our Father because by His Providence He cares for us and provides us with everything we need.

- He is our Father because He has prepared for us a share in the inheritance that awaits us if we are faithful to the inspirations of His grace.

Christ made sure that from the opening invocation to the closing petition, we realized our solidarity with others. The collective words "we," "our," and "us" occur nine times in the Lord's Prayer. This emphasizes the fact that the followers of Christ form a spiritual family, that we are members of the human race, and that when we pray we should recognize our kinship with others and other people's need of our prayerful help.

Whenever Christ spoke to His heavenly Father, He always said "My Father." There is only one natural Father of the Second Person of the Trinity. To bring this truth home, Christ also had no natural father of His human nature. But when Jesus taught us to pray, He told *us* to address God as *our* Father.

Saying to God, "who art in heaven", does not mean that somehow He is not on earth. But He is in heaven as the Destiny to which He is calling us and for which we were made.

In a mysterious sense, heaven is wherever the experience of God's presence is enjoyed. On earth we have a foretaste of heaven in the joy that God gives to those who serve Him, even while they carry their daily cross. In eternity this joy will be unalloyed and without sorrow or any trial.

The visible "heavens" of sky and sun, moon and stars are the biblical symbol for "heaven" as the home where God dwells and where Christ is preparing a place for us. The opening words of the Lord's

Prayer are, therefore, a reminder to raise our minds and hearts from the things below to those which are above. Everything on earth should be seen as a means to the end, or goal, which is our heavenly reward.

FIRST PETITION:
"HALLOWED BE THY NAME"

The Latin words of the first petition bring out clearly what we are here asking for: "Sanctificetur Nomen tuum."

What we are asking is that the Name of God may be sanctified. This calls for some explanations. We are not asking that God might become more holy. That would be blasphemy. He is the All-Holy One because He is the Totally Other. He alone is the Necessary One, the Infinite One; there is no other God than He.

Our petition is rather that God might be recognized and served as God by us and in us. He *is* all powerful, all wise, and all good. He *is* the Creator and the Destiny of the human race. But not everyone either acknowledges Him for who He is, or serves Him as He deserves.

Yet that is the main reason why God created rational human beings. He wants them to know Him—love and serve Him in time—as the condition for possessing him in eternity.

In biblical language, "name" means the being

who is named. When we pray that the name of God may be sanctified, we are asking that He may be glorified by His human creatures because they are His children and He is their God.

In the Church's understanding, the comparison which occurs in the third petition, "on earth as it is in heaven," refers to all the first three petitions. Consequently, in asking that the name of God be hallowed—that God may be known and loved—we are really praying that His name may be as hallowed on earth as it is in heaven.

If we ask, how is God's name hallowed in heaven? the answer is clear. He is hallowed in heaven perfectly. The angels and saints in heaven know Him to perfection and they love Him to the limit of their created power.

Our petition, then, is that we on earth might grow in our knowledge and love of God. Every day, and in fact, every moment, our loving knowledge or intelligent love of Him should become more and more like the beatific vision of the hosts of heaven.

One more observation. The more we sanctify the name of God, by our devoted service, the more He will sanctify us. Indeed, we may say that our sanctity depends on how devotedly we hallow the name of God.

Second Petition:
"Thy Kingdom Come"

The kingdom for which we are praying to come is the kingdom of which Christ so constantly spoke in the gospels. The Greek word *Basileia* (kingdom), which occurs in the Lord's Prayer is the same term He used throughout His public ministry and, after the Resurrection, up to the time of His ascension into heaven.

Jesus intended us to pray that the kingdom He described, in every sense, might come.

There are two principal ways in which Jesus spoke of the kingdom. He described it as a present reality, and as a future anticipation.

Present Reality

The kingdom as a present reality is the Church which Christ was founding. It is a visible reality to which people are called by the preaching of the gospel; into which they enter through Baptism; in which they are sanctified by the sacraments; which is composed of both good and bad members; with which

Christ identifies Himself as "my kingdom"; and from which the whole world receives the graces of salvation.

On all these levels, the kingdom as present reality is meant to "come," that is, to increase and intensify.

- We pray that the Church may become more effective in proclaiming the gospel; that the zeal of her members might increase by spending themselves in preaching Christ and Him crucified.

- We pray that more people may receive the gift of the true faith and be baptized.

- We pray that those who are in the Church may become more holy and pleasing to God.

- We pray that those in the Church who are estranged from God through sin may repent and be reconciled with the Lord.

- We pray that Christians may become more Christlike so that others may see their good works and be drawn to embrace the faith that produces such reflections of the Divine Master.

- We pray that by their practice of virtue, all followers may become more effective channels of grace to everyone whose life they touch.

Future Anticipation

Especially in the Gospel of Matthew, Jesus speaks frequently of the "kingdom of heaven."

Here the petition of the Lord's Prayer is a plea for the salvation of souls and for their glorification in the world to come.

- We pray for the grace that people need to reach the heavenly kingdom for which they were made.

- We pray for the light that people need to know God's will in their lives and the strength to fulfill this will, so they may deserve to enter heaven.

- We pray that those who belong to Christ's kingdom on earth may be more generous in cooperating with His grace, so that in heaven they may give God greater glory for all eternity.

THIRD PETITION:
"THY WILL BE DONE ON EARTH AS IT IS IN HEAVEN"

This petition is an epitome of Christianity and a synthesis of our whole purpose for existence.

Why do we have a free will? In order to do the will of God. Unlike the irrational creation that surrounds us, we can choose either to conform our wills to God or refuse to do so.

The scope of this petition is the prayer that human beings on earth might do God's will as the angels and saints are doing in heaven. We therefore ask that everyone on earth may do God's will, even as everyone in heaven does. There are no exceptions in heaven. We pray that there will be fewer and fewer exceptions in doing God's will on earth.

We further ask that, as in heaven, people may do God's will out of love and not through fear. In heaven there is no danger of not doing God's will, and therefore no fear of the consequences.

We further pray that we on earth, like those in heaven, may do God's will spontaneously. We ask that the divine will be done without hesitation, with no aversion or reluctance. On earth we know how slow we can be in responding to the known will of God. Our plea is to become more ready to fulfill the will of God the moment we know what He wants.

We also pray to do God's will with selfless generosity. There is no envy in heaven among the elect, because they see others also doing God's will. There is no jealousy but perfect cooperation in performing the divine will, not only individually but collectively.

We finally pray that, as in heaven, those on earth may enjoy doing the will of God. There is a mysterious relationship between our doing what pleases God, and God's doing what pleases us. In heaven, everyone does only what pleases God. He, in turn, does everything to please the elect. They are supremely happy. Why? Because they are perfectly conformed to the will of the Most High. We pray to discover, already on earth, a foretaste of the joys of heaven, reserved for those who do the divine will. In fact, the measure of true happiness this side of heaven is the degree of our fidelity in doing the divine will.

FOURTH PETITION:
"GIVE US THIS DAY OUR DAILY BREAD"

This is the turning point in the Our Father. Where the first three petitions were directed to the glory of God, from now on they are concerned with our needs.

The Church's tradition finds two levels of request for nourishment in this petition. We ask for the food we need for our souls, and the sustenance we need for our bodies.

Spiritual Nourishment

When St. Pius X issued his decree on frequent Holy Communion, he explained that frequent means daily reception of the Blessed Sacrament. He based his teaching on the comparison with the food that we daily need to sustain our bodies, and the "all but unanimous interpretation" of the Fathers of the Church. They say that "daily bread" in the Lord's Prayer means daily Communion. The pope concludes that "the Eucharistic Bread should be our daily food."

It is assumed that, in receiving Holy Communion, a person has sanctifying grace. The reason is obvious. No less than food for the body presumes that the body has its natural life, so the Eucharistic food for the soul presumes that the soul is supernaturally alive.

There is also another spiritual food that we pray for in this petition. That is the nourishment of truth that the human mind needs for its daily sustenance. No less than the body needs material food to remain healthy and stay alive, so the soul has to be fed daily on God's revealed word to maintain its spiritual vigor and life.

Christ's long discourse on the promise of the Eucharist uses the same word "Bread" to refer to both kinds of spiritual nourishment: His own living Body in the Holy Eucharist, and His revealed word in the truths of salvation.

Daily Needs of the Body

On the material side of our bodily needs, the fourth petition asks God to provide the hungry with food, the homeless with shelter, the sick and the aged with adequate care, the victims of addiction to drugs and alcohol with help to recover from indulgence and the resulting disease.

This petition applies to both impoverished and

affluent societies, which often co-exist in the same country and even the same city or locality.

It is no exaggeration to say that in praying "Give us this day our daily bread" we are literally begging the Lord to move the hearts of men to share with one another of the resources that He makes available for respectable human living.

It is a sad irony of the modern world in an age of unprecedented wealth, the world is going through a period of superhuman suffering. There are many reasons for this paradox. But one of them is the cold indifference to the bodily sufferings of countless millions in every region of the globe.

When Pope John Paul II wrote his apostolic exhortation on *The Christian Meaning of Human Suffering*, he touched on every aspect of this petition of the Our Father.

We are to pray, he said, especially that God in His mercy, will inspire a legion of Good Samaritans to see the physical needs of other people and come to their selfless aid.

Following the parable of the Gospel, we could say that suffering, which is present under so many different forms in our human world, is also present in order to unleash love in the human person, that unselfish gift of one's "I" on behalf of other people, especially those who suffer. . . .

The world of human suffering calls for, so to speak, another world: the world of human love; and in a certain sense owes to suffering that unselfish love which stirs in one's heart and actions.

The person who is a "neighbor" cannot indifferently pass by the suffering of another. . . .

He must "stop," "sympathize" just like the Samaritan in the gospel parable. The parable in itself expresses a deeply Christian truth, but one that at the same time is very universally human. It is not without reason that, also in ordinary speech any activity on behalf of the suffering and needy is called "Good Samaritan" work (*Salvifici doloris*, VII, 29).

Whatever else we pray for, when we ask for our daily bread, we are asking the God of mercy to inspire countless Good Samaritans to reflect this mercy in their loving concern for the suffering of others.

FIFTH PETITION:
"FORGIVE US OUR TRESPASSES AS WE FORGIVE THOSE WHO TRESPASS AGAINST US"

This is no ordinary petition to God asking for His mercy. We not only ask Him to be merciful to us, but we dare place a condition and a norm on God's forgiveness. What is this condition and norm? It is the practice and the measure of our forgiveness to others.

What are we being told? We are being told that unless we are merciful to others, God will not be merciful to us. We further believe that the measure of our forbearance with the sins of others mysteriously determines the degree of God's patient forgiveness of us.

Every form of mercy that we so deeply desire from God toward ourselves, we pray that we might receive from Him. But the condition remains. God will infallibly be tolerant and patient, indulgent and lenient, tender and compassionate, pardoning and forgiving toward us sinners if we practice these qualities of mercy toward those whom God's Providence puts into our lives.

St. Matthew speaks of "debts" and "debtors," St. Luke of "sins" and being "indebted." But the mean-

323

ing in each case is clear. By offending God in sin, we incur a debt of love and punishment for our misdeeds. We owe God greater love than we would have had we not sinned, and we owe Him a debt of suffering as punishment for offending the Divine Majesty.

In His mercy, God provides us with countless opportunities for expiation by allowing others to sin against us. Our patience in enduring their offenses, our kindness in bearing their coldness, our responding with love for them in return for their lovelessness toward us is part of God's providential plan of redeeming a sinful world.

We pray for the strength to forgive so that we might be forgiven in return.

There is also a marvelous communication of grace at stake here. Not infrequently, the very reason God places difficult people into our lives is that by our loving patience with them, we might obtain from God the graces of conversion they need. We *are* channels of grace to others. This means that to be an effective channel for some people, I may have to be the victim of their indifference, or even cruelty, to win for them the gift of repentance to be reconciled with an offended God.

SIXTH PETITION:
"LEAD US NOT INTO TEMPTATION"

Temptation is an invitation to sin. The source of the temptation may be the attractive, sinful conduct of other people, called the world; or the disorderly desires of our own fallen nature called concupiscence; or the malicious urging of the evil spirit, whom we call the devil.

When we pray not to be led into temptation, we are not asking to be freed from the testing of all human beings to prove their loyalty to God. Temptation as a test of our fidelity to Him is part of our probation here on earth, and the price of earning our reward in the world to come.

What we are praying for is not to allow ourselves to give in to temptation, but rather to profit from the temptation experience. The saintly interpreters of the Lord's Prayer give no less than nine ways that we should protect ourselves from yielding to temptation and should profit from the inevitable temptations in our lives. Our prayer in this petition will be answered to the extent that we follow these rules of Christian wisdom:

1. Be on guard against the evil spirit. Know his strategy, be able to recognize his deceits and above all, "resist him, steadfast in the faith" (I Peter 5:9).

2. Daily examine your conscience to see how well you coped with the temptations of each day. Thank God for the grace of benefiting from the temptations you overcame, and ask His forgiveness for those to which you gave in.

3. Periodically, during the day, look into the "book of your soul." Read there what thoughts are on your mind, what desires in your will. Sift these interior movements by discarding some, keeping others, and acting on those which your conscience tells you are graces from God.

4. Be suspicious of your natural tendency to go after whatever appeals to you. Avoid being impulsive in rejecting what you dislike, or embracing what you like. All temptations are attractive. Learn to practice discernment of spirits as explained by the masters of the spiritual life.

5. Remember that we are now living by faith, which means that of ourselves we may not even recognize a temptation. Thus we must constantly ask for light from God: "Lord, that I may see."

6. Life on earth is a warfare and we are members of the Church Militant. We must, therefore, be properly armed with humility and prudence, and the graces that come for the asking. Christ's admonition to the disciples in Gethsemane is ad-

dressed to all of us, "Watch and pray, that you may not enter into temptation" (Matthew 26:41).

7. Be on the alert. We can get into habits of action that may dull our perception. Custom can blind us to danger and keep us from even knowing we are being tempted. We may give in before we even realize what has happened.

8. Set yourself models for imitation. Do not follow the crowd. Come to know certain persons whose conduct you admire and whose example you resolve to follow. It may be several people. In one you imitate the person's humility, in another fidelity to prayer, in another selfless charity, in another uncomplaining patience, in another cheerfulness under trial, in another prudent planning of work, in another devotion to the Eucharist, in another a great love of Mary, and in another a strong zeal for souls. In this way, we have a ready substitute for the temptations from the world—the attractive sinful behavior of others. We have, instead, the inspiration of good people in the world—their attractive practice of virtue.

9. Do not live in false security. Cultivate a healthy fear of offending a loving God. This will give you the protection you need to remain faithful to Him no matter how seductive the temptations you encounter.

SEVENTH PETITION:
"DELIVER US FROM EVIL. AMEN"

The closing petition of the Lord's Prayer is a compendium of everything from which we want God to deliver us, in this life and in the life to come.

St. Cyprian, who wrote the first extensive commentary on the *Pater Noster*, teaches that we are here praying to be freed from the consequences of sin. The Church follows this teaching, which places our dread of evil into proper perspective.

So far, in the Our Father, we have prayed for God's mercy on our sins, for strength to do God's will, for wisdom not to give into temptations. In closing, we ask to be spared such evils as are the result of sin, our own and the sins of others.

Evil, in general, is anything contrary to the will. But there are two kinds of evil, even as there are, finally, two wills that can be displeased. That which is contrary to God's will we call sin. That which is contrary to the human will we call pain.

The special focus of the last petition of the Lord's Prayer is to be delivered from pain. But, immediately we must be careful to explain what this means.

While ultimately all pain is somehow the result of sin, not all pain is bad for us. Indeed some pain is even necessary for the salvation and sanctification of the world.

When God became man, He had joy set before Him and chose the Cross. If we are to become like Him and cooperate with Him in the redemption of the world, we should expect and even embrace a certain amount of pain in our lives.

Yet in the final petition of His own prayer, Christ tells us to ask for deliverance from evil. What kind of evil, as pain, are we praying to be spared? Pain is whatever contradicts our wills. It can be pain in the body, or pain in the soul. It can be physical distress or emotional disturbance, or spiritual dryness, or mental anxiety. In a word, the pain can be anything, inside of us or outside of us, that we find displeasing and want to be freed from enduring.

Realizing that pain can be a great blessing, we pray to be delivered from such pain as God, in His wisdom, knows would not be beneficial for our souls. We also pray to profit from the pain we have to suffer. We pray that the pain we endure will benefit others. And we pray for deliverance from that absolute evil which is the eternal loss of God.

"Amen" is considered part of the biblical text of the Lord's Prayer. It is in the Latin Vulgate of the New Testament and has been extensively commented on by the saints.

Literally "Amen" means, "truly," or "it is true," and expresses acceptance of what has just been said. At the end of the Our Father it is an earnest hope that God will grant all our preceding petitions. It is an act of confidence that the Father is moved by this "Amen," which Jesus so often used to stress the divine authority of His words.

About the Author

John A. Hardon, S.J., is a member of the Society of Jesus. Father Hardon holds a master's degree in philosophy from Loyola University in Chicago and a doctorate in theology from the Gregorian University in Rome. He has taught at the Jesuit School of Theology in Chicago and the Institute for Advanced Studies in Catholic Doctrine at St. John's University in New York, as well as helped organize and publish the *Christ Our Life* series of religion books for elementary schools and Confraternity of Christian Doctrine programs. A prolific writer, whose works have appeared in leading religious and educational periodicals as well as various collections, he has authored many books, including: *The Catholic Catechism, Religions of the World, Protestant Churches of America, Christianity in the Twentieth Century, Theology of Prayer, Modern Catholic Dictionary,* and *The Treasury of Catholic Wisdom.* In addition, he is actively involved with a number of organizations, including the Institute on Religious Life, the Apostolate for Family Consecration, the Catholic Home Study Institute, and the Marian Catechists. Until recently,

Father Hardon divided his time between New York, Chicago, and Washington, D.C., writing and teaching theology. He now concentrates on the writing apostolate for international evangelization and catechesis. He resides at the University of Detroit.

INDEX

Index

Index

335

Index